The Great Inflation

The
Great Inflation

Germany 1919-23

William Guttmann
and
Patricia Meehan

SAXON  HOUSE

SAXON HOUSE, D. C. Heath Ltd,
Westmead, Farnborough, Hants, England

ISBN 0 347 00017 7

Library of Congress Catalog Card Number 74-24312

Printed and bound in Great Britain by
REDWOOD BURN LIMITED
Trowbridge & Esher

Contents

Authors' Acknowledgement

We wish to acknowledge with gratitude the generous help and co-operation of the many men and women who, having lived through the grim period of history with which this book is concerned, shared the memory of their experiences with us, either by letter or in personal interviews.

All the documentary sources used are set out at the end of the book.

Introduction

In the Germany of the year 1923 it was clear, even to the most unworldly, that something mysterious and frightening was happening. Money as one of the foundations of society was dying, and its death was producing chaos, despair and a sort of collective insanity.

We call that period of history the "great German Inflation", and its story, which is the theme of this book, is, in the words of Viscount D'Abernon, British Ambassador in Germany at the time, one of those "tales of wonder and adventure which owe their interest to the extravagances of the facts recounted".

Inflation and the depreciation of money is an age-old phenomenon. But never in the history of mankind has it reached such bewildering dimensions as in Germany in the years that followed the country's defeat in the First World War. There was a brief inflationary spasm in Hungary in 1946 which for a time exceeded the German inflation, but it was restricted in its effects and historically negligible.

The very magnitude of the figures has caught the

imagination of people all over the world. By the end of 1923, the banknotes in circulation represented a nominal value of the staggering sum of about 500 trillion (500,000,000,000,000,000,000) paper marks; and the value of the German currency unit, the mark, had fallen to one billionth of its pre-war value: it took 1 billion* paper marks to equal the value of one gold mark. Figures carrying a dozen noughts were part of daily life.

The great German Inflation naturally became the subject of sociological and economic studies, but it was more than a financial phenomenon. Such well-known authors as Thomas Mann, Stefan Zweig, Hans Fallada and others introduced it into their works of fiction. It has entered folklore and legend and even now conjures up in the minds of quite ordinary folk pictures of people carrying laundry baskets full of worthless banknotes, of beggars being given potato sacks full of paper marks yet unable to buy with the gift even a piece of bread.

A story is told of two women carrying to the bank a laundry basket filled to the brim with banknotes. Seeing a crowd standing round a shop window, they put down their basket for a moment to see if there was anything that they could buy. When they turned round a few moments later, they found the money still there untouched. But the basket had gone.

The collapse of the German currency all but ruined the

---

*Although modern practice tends to use the term "billion" for 1,000 millions, we follow the system current in Germany during the Inflation and in the currency, documents and literature pertaining to the period; i.e. 1 billion = 1 million millions (1,000,000,000,000), 1 trillion = 1 million billions (1,000,000,000,000,000,000), etc. The term "milliard" stands for 1,000 millions.

fabric of German society, produced a social revolution, and was at least partly responsible for the country's political development culminating in the rise of Nazism. Hitler has been called the foster child of the Inflation.

. It left a permanent mark on the psyche of the nation, with far-reaching effects that the passing of time has not been able to eradicate completely. Thus, on various subsequent occasions, the mere fear of inflation which the trauma of the nineteen-twenties had implanted in the minds of the German people was responsible for policies and attitudes, sometimes for better, sometimes for worse. In 1924, for instance, it helped to create the spirit of restraint and self-denial needed to maintain the stability recently brought to the currency. Conversely, during the world economic crisis of the nineteen-thirties, it prevented the German authorities from applying even mildly inflationary policies, which might have made the recession less disastrous.

After the Second World War, the memory of inflation can safely be said to have induced, in the working classes of the West German Federal Republic, that moderation in their wage claims which played an important part in the economic recovery of their country — the legendary "German economic miracle". And it was the great German Inflation that had the doubtful merit of making "inflation" a household word, all too familiar to everyone, young and old, rich and poor.

Today "inflation" is fast becoming a universal obsession. It means, according to the Oxford English Dictionary, "a great and undue expansion or enlargement, an enlargement, an increase beyond proper limits"; in monetary terms, a proliferation of money closely connected with an upsurge of prices.

It took a long time for this to enter the consciousness

of the German people. When, as a result of the First World War, prices in Germany began to rise steeply, the talk was of the increasing cost of living and the need for tightening one's belt. An article in the *Kölnische Zeitung* of 4th March 1922 is typical of those appearing in the German press at the time; it observed that, the price of shoes having reached 550, and a man's suit 3–4,000, marks, the wave of high prices had turned into a flood. Newspapers complained about high prices and demanded remedies for the rising cost of living without the word "inflation" ever being mentioned. Indeed, as long as inflation and the decline in the real value of money were not recognised as such, the situation was not without its economically beneficial aspects: it induced saving, capital accumulation for investment, and thus economic growth.

Only when people became aware that what had happened had been a decline in the value of money did the word "inflation" enter the everday language. Awareness of the phenomenon turned the will to save and to accumulate capital into its exact opposite.

One has only to glance at today's newspapers, with the frequent mention of "inflation" in editorials, news and advertising columns, to recognise that it has indeed travelled far. But on its long journey through time and space it has acquired many more facets. The doctrines evolved around it have become more subtle and sophisticated. There is a vast and growing literature on the nature of inflation, its causes and cures.

The argument centres around the interplay of inflation and the supply of money. The supporters of the quantity, or monetarist, theory maintain, in the words of the economist Professor H. G. Johnson, that "inflation is associated with, and ultimately causally dependent on, a rate of increase of the money supply significantly in excess of the rate of growth of real output — the difference between the two rates being the rate of inflation". Others shift the emphasis away from the money supply and question its importance in the problem.

This is not the place to pronounce on the validity of the contrasting opinions or to go into the details of the controversy, which continues with the ascendancy now of one side, now of the other. For the present purpose it is sufficient briefly and in general terms to define some of the points that are relevant to the development of our theme.

Inflation, then, is a phenomenon concerned with the relationship between the quantity of money available for the purchase of goods and services and the quantity and the price of goods and services available to be so purchased. If the total amount of available goods and services contracts without the amount of purchasing power also being reduced, then, in the now classic phrase, "too much money is chasing too few goods". The general level of prices will rise and the value of money will deteriorate. The same result will occur if additional money is put into circulation or if the circulation of existing money becomes more rapid by an increase in purchases — a "spending spree" — without the amount of purchasable goods being increased.

The inflationary spiral may be triggered off by a scarcity of goods related to an excess of demand ("demand-pull" inflation); or it may be triggered off by a rise in costs, such as higher wages and salaries resulting in increased purchasing power, not accompanied by higher productivity ("cost-push" inflation). Thus money inflation and price inflation are not necessarily co-existent. They are not co-existent if, owing to increased productivity, the increased quantity of money is balanced by an increased Gross National Product. Hence the frequency of combining agreements on wage increases with productivity deals in an attempt to stave off price increases.

Whatever the particular character of the inflation, its essence is continual movement — upwards. This momentum is kept up and accelerated by the anticipation of its persistence: the anticipation of higher prices quickens the demand for goods and leads to even higher prices; the anticipation of a higher cost of living stimulates the demand for higher wages; and the anticipation of higher costs in general induces the producer as well as the trader to add an extra charge to the prices of his merchandise in order to cover himself against the expected higher cost of their replacement.

Inflation is not an Act of God. Unlike natural disasters, such as floods, drought, earthquakes and crop failures, which can change the economic conditions of nations, inflation is man-made and can be started, prevented, regulated and stopped by human action. Purchasing power can be skimmed off by taxation; prices and wages can be controlled, savings encouraged. Inversely, governments can increase purchasing power by boosting their expenditure through public works, defence spending, higher government salaries, wages, pensions and so on, aiming in this way at influencing the relationship between money and prices. They can inflate, reflate, refuel the economy or damp down overheating. Governments, however, are not almighty; their decisions will be the result of a struggle between those who have an interest in inflation and those who prefer a stable currency.

Whether they intend to inflate or deflate, they are subject to pressures from their own citizens or foreigners, from trades unions and employers, from speculators and others, and much depends upon what those forces demand and are able to achieve.

For inflation is not an unmitigated evil. An advertisement by an assurance company, in *The Observer* of 6th March 1973, was headed "Inflation could lead to you being better off", illustrating the point that some, at least, are persuaded that inflation is a blessing.

Indeed, as long as inflation is moderate (and some have suggested a distinction between inflation that can be beneficial and hyper-inflation, which, like the great German Inflation in its last stages, leads to disaster), it will usually stimulate the national economy, for once people are aware of inflation and expect prices to rise the next day, they will naturally tend to make their purchases immediately and thus increase the volume of trade and production, and the greater quantity of goods on offer may even result in steadying the price level. In this way the national economy as a whole will benefit. On the other hand, the advantages deriving from inflation may be confined to groups powerful enough to exert their influence in favour of continuing and growing inflation.

The effects of the great German Inflation were, for most of its duration, determined by a principle expressed in the simple formula "mark equals mark". In other words, the mark, whatever its intrinsic value might be, remained the legal currency unit for the purpose of all money transactions. Thus, an obligation expressed in x marks could be discharged by the payment of x marks, however diminished its value due to inflation, and the creditor would have to accept such a payment as full settlement.

The Great Inflation

The real victims of this disastrous state of affairs were the owners of capital assets in marks (such as cash, life insurances and state securities); those, like pensioners, who had to live on fixed incomes; and, in general, all those who did not have the power of pressing for an increase in their income commensurate with the sinking value of money. Even workers who benefited from the stimulating effect of inflation simply by being kept employed suffered, in varying degrees according to the greater or lesser pressure they were able to exert. As the Organisation for Economic Co-operation and Development said, in its *Economic Outlook* of 20th July 1973, "High inflation entails distortions of income and wealth patterns which are not only unfair but produce continuous social strains."

Indeed the worst, the near-fatal aspect of the great German Inflation was the resulting inequalities, hardships and social upheavals and changes. It is only fair to note in passing that in the inflationary conditions of today some lessons have been learned, perhaps from the German precedent. For instance, the more equitable harmonisation of social security pensions with the depreciation of the currency (practised in many countries, but characteristically brought to a high degree of refinement by the German Federal Republic, in its scheme for "dynamisation of pensions") is effective in at least mitigating the worst ravages of inflation.

Besides the relationship between the supply of money, the supply of goods and services, and the level of prices, there is another relationship of importance to any consideration of the problem of inflation: that between the internal value of a currency (its purchasing power at home) and its external value (its purchasing power abroad). This is basically expressed in the rate of exchange on the international exchange market, the rate itself being closely connected with the state of balance of payments. (As the Inflation in Germany progressed, the exchange rate with the dollar became the yardstick for measuring the degree of the mark's inflation, as well as its internal value.) Indeed, the interaction of rising prices and a falling exchange rate is typical of a "classical" inflation.

The exchange rate of a currency, as the experience of the last few years reminds us, can be fixed in relation either to gold or to other currencies and be kept stable by various devices; or it can be adjusted from time to time, either upward (as has happened recently with the revaluations of the Deutschmark) or downward (as with the devaluations of the pound sterling). Again, the currency may be allowed to float upward or downward according to the day-to-day vagaries of the international exchange markets. The essential point to be made about the behaviour of the mark during the great German Inflation is that it was floating freely all the time, sometimes upward, but usually downward, and the downward movement became, as time went on, a headlong plunge. This fact was of great importance to the degree of discrepancy between the internal and external values of the German currency.

Generally speaking, the price of a currency is determined by the economic rules of supply and demand, including speculative supply and demand, which in turn may be influenced by economic, political and psychological factors and the anticipation of these. If a country makes payments abroad in excess of payments it receives, for instance if its imports exceed its exports — as was the case with Germany in the years after the First World War, the exigencies of the war having resulted in a lack of goods and raw materials — or if it has to make unilateral transfers, as Germany did in the form of reparations, the demand for foreign currency will drive up its price. As just such circumstances prevailed in the nineteen-twenties, the value of the mark fell, and this in turn made German goods cheaper to foreign buyers. There followed what we should term an "export-led" boom, which, while it helped to keep the German economy busy, did not stop the downward movement of the mark or the speculation that contributed to its difficulties.

Pressure on the mark was aggravated by financial policies. The expenditure of the German government, quite apart from reparations payments, rose to unprecedented heights. Tax receipts were quite insufficient to cover it, and the remainder was supplied by borrowing and by a flood of paper money from the printing press. It was this paper money that ultimately depreciated to a point where the currency collapsed and died.

In the late stages of the great German Inflation all the elements that have been mentioned — the dollar rate, rising prices, government spending and increased money circulation — combined to form a veritable vicious circle. As the exchange rate of the mark fell, prices responded automatically and so did wages and salaries. This in its turn induced increased government spending and the issue of even more banknotes; and the resulting flood of paper from the printing presses caused a further fall in the mark rate. It was the dance of death for the mark and the German economy.

In these introductory pages we have briefly explained the meaning of the word "inflation". Part I of the book sets the scene, telling the story of the Inflation chronologically in its historical context: what happened and why. The actual course of the Inflation is charted as it accelerates, spins away into disaster and, almost overnight, comes to an end.

But the deeper meaning of inflation does not emerge from cold facts and economic analysis alone. The great Inflation in Germany was, as indeed inflation is today, the warp and woof of daily life, and it is with the human aspect of such inflation that our book is also concerned. In making so much use of personal recollections obtained by interviews and letters, our purpose is to tell how that dramatic and traumatic experience affected the German people; to look at it through the eyes of some of those who, because they lived through it, are able to convey that "tale of wonder and adventure" in human terms. When all is said and done, these are the only terms that matter.

PART I

PART I

The Road to Ruin

In the classic words of the advice Marshal Trivulzio gave
to his master, King Louis XII of France, "There are three
things you need to wage war: money, money, and more
money." To wage the war that engulfed Europe in 1914
required a very great deal of money indeed.

Wars have a way of producing inflation. A nation at
war has to divert its resources and to spend a fabulous
sum of money to keep its armies supplied and to satisfy
their insatiable appetite for the weapons of destruction,
which are themselves destined to be destroyed. As these
go up in the smoke of the battlefields and have to be
replaced again and again, money pours out to pay for the
wasteful and unproductive war effort, while the ordinary
needs of the economy have to take second place. The
consequence is, that the demand for scarce and urgently
needed goods drives prices up and more money has to be
created to meet them. This is the climate in which
inflation flourishes.

True to tradition, the great German Inflation started
almost exactly at the moment the First World War broke
out.

The Great Inflation

Before the fateful August of 1914, the civilised world had lived under the gold standard in a golden age in which a smoothly working system assured, almost without exception, the stability of prices and exchange rates.

Germany, an industrial power ranking high among the trading nations and, in consequence, extremely prosperous, had until then lived under the monetary rules laid down by the Bank Law of 1875. The central bank, the Reichsbank, issued the money required by the economy, and the stability of the currency in circulation was secured by ensuring that a third of the total was backed up by gold, and the remaining two thirds by commercial bills guaranteed by persons of proven solvency. The number of commercial bills taken up by the bank was logically in proportion to the activity of the economy — the resulting circulation expanding or shrinking in accord with the demands of the market. In other words, the money in circulation represented either gold or what later became referred to as *Sachwerte* — the actual goods that had been exchanged for the bills in the bank's portfolio.

The outbreak of war immediately confronted the German economy with a critical situation. The blockade of the country imposed by the Allies all but killed the international trade on which it had come to rely so much for its prosperity. It was cut off from the sources of most of the imported food and raw materials needed to ensure the productivity and welfare of the nation.

Oddly enough, the Germans, for all their proverbial thoroughness, had not made any provisions or plans for such a contingency. Yet perhaps this was not so odd, for, in common with the other belligerents, Germany believed firmly that the war — the first modern war in which the achievements of war technology were to be used on a massive scale with all the array of deadly weapons, from the super guns like the Big Bertha to Zeppelins, aircraft and poison gas — would be a short one. The slogan "Home by Christmas" was not peculiar to any one of the warring nations. Of course, the Germans thought it would end in victory for them, and victory would solve all the problems.

Germany's certainty of victory was naturally based on her military readiness and planning, which, in contrast to what had been done in the purely economic field, was meticulous. It was confidently expected that the war would be won long before any economic troubles could develop.

Naturally, German planners counted money as a type of ammunition, and the mobilisation of financial resources was planned in the same way as its military counterpart. In 1905 an international crisis had arisen over the question of which European powers should play a dominating rôle in Morocco. Germany felt slighted by certain Anglo-French arrangements and the danger of a conflagration seemed imminent. This was followed by a second Moroccan crisis in 1911. It was in that context that Rudolf Havenstein, the man who as President of the Reichsbank was the protagonist in the tragedy of the great German Inflation, drew up the financial contingency plans for war.

When, at the end of July 1914, the war fever reached its height and the great powers began to mobilise their armies, certain sections of the German public began to panic and started a run on the Reichsbank to convert their money into gold, as they were then entitled to do under existing legislation. The gold reserves were rapidly drained of over 100 million marks. That was the danger signal; but though, from 31st July onwards, the banks in fact refused to exchange notes for gold coins, it was not until 4th August, when war had been declared and the Reichstag met to put into execution the plans for financial mobilisation in wartime, that legislation was passed to abolish convertibility into gold. That was the opening of the path to inflation.

The German government decided to finance the war by borrowing, and its cynical justification for this decision was that the beaten enemy would pay for everything. Karl Helfferich, Secretary to the Treasury, declared, in a speech before the Reichstag, "After the war we shall not forgo . . . our claim that our enemies shall make restitution for all the material damage (quite apart from everything else) they have caused by the irresponsible launching of the war against us."

The Reichstag approved war credits to the amount of 5,000 million marks. At the same time it was decreed that, henceforward, three-month Treasury bills would be allowed to play the same rôle as commercial bills, namely to serve as backing for the issue of banknotes. In fact, the Reichsbank was authorised to take up and discount unlimited amounts of these Treasury bills (which, unlike the commercial bills, did not represent any underlying *Sachwerte*, but simply government obligations, bonds, sold to the Bank and enabling it to create money). In addition, so-called *Darlehnskassen* (loan banks) were set up for the purpose of giving credit and issuing currency in the form of *Darlehnskassenscheine* (loan-bank notes) to circulate side by side with the notes issued by the Reichsbank. All these new credit instruments were considered as "backing" for the issue of notes — indeed, the Reichsbank was proud to maintain that the paper money in circulation was properly backed according to the law.

Thus, with the notes issued on the strength of the Treasury bills and the loan-bank credits, the inflation of the currency showed up very early. On 7th August 1914 the amount of money in circulation was 2,000 million marks higher than it had been two weeks before.

In passing, it is interesting to note what happened to the gold coins. Difficult though it is to imagine now, in pre-1914 Europe gold pieces circulated freely as ordinary money; in Germany, 10 or 20 mark gold coins were almost considered a nuisance on account of their weight. Not only did the Reichsbank suspend the convertibility — that is, the sale — of gold, but strenuous efforts were also made to draw as many gold coins as possible out of circulation or private hoards and redirect them into the coffers of the Reichsbank. A vast propaganda machine was set in motion for this purpose with appeals to the patriotism of the citizens — "The gold belongs to the Reichsbank" — and schoolboys were proud of receiving solemn certificates acknowledging that they had collected and delivered to the Reichsbank so many thousands in gold and deserved well of the Fatherland.

Later, patriotism was not enough to ensure the inflow of gold coins, and drastic measures were taken: soldiers, for instance, were promised extra leave in return for the delivery of so many gold coins, something unheard of in militarist Germany. The idea behind this was quite simple: in the first years of the war, a third of the value of banknotes had to be backed by its equivalent in gold, so that, for every 20 gold-mark piece the Reichsbank took in, it was entitled to issue 60 paper marks — a procedure that was not thought likely to endanger the stability of the currency.

Germany's total expenditure during the First World

The Great Inflation

War amounted to the colossal sum of 164,000 million marks, some 147,000 millions of which represented the actual cost of the war. Against this, the accounts show a total income of 121,000 million marks, which leaves a gap of some 40,000 millions, covered by Treasury bills. Some of these bills ended up in the hands of banks, institutions and other bodies, but the remainder were discounted by the Reichsbank, which in turn issued paper money. By the end of 1918, the amount of money in circulation had reached the sum of 35,000 million marks, about five times as much as before the war.

As for the above-mentioned "income", a full 100,000 million marks of this derived from the proceeds of several issues of war loan, which were made at regular intervals, beginning in September 1914. The first four issues, which still benefited from spontaneous or propaganda-inspired patriotic fervour, were successful in mopping up the purchasing power created by the Treasury bills and the ensuing increased circulation of money. (In 1916, the Treasury bills discounted by the Reichsbank amounted to nearly 9,000 million marks' worth, and the currency in circulation had approximately doubled.) But it became increasingly difficult to keep up the public investment in war loans, quite apart from the fact that the ever-rising nominal amounts of successive loans did not compensate for the lower real value of the inflow. The government had to exert more and more pressure to persuade such public bodies as savings banks and local authorities to do their patriotic duty; and they did this, not having sufficient funds of their own, by borrowing on the security of bonds they had had to take up in the past, and merrily adding their own deficit spending to that of the Reich. From the fifth war loan onwards, the proceeds from the subscriptions were regularly less than the value of the Treasury bills issued, and the resulting difference could not fail to exert further inflationary pressure. Shortly before the end of the war, the deficit — that is, the unfunded indebtedness of the Reich — was in the region of 50,000 million marks.

In these circumstances the government retracted its promise to finance the war entirely by borrowing and not by taxation. From 1916 onwards several Acts were promulgated instituting some new direct and indirect taxes, among them taxes on war profits, coal and transport, and a turnover tax. But the results were disappointing, partly owing to the low rates of taxation, due perhaps to the fact that the government only half-heartedly agreed to modify its principles. The total revenue from taxation, old as well as new, was not even sufficient to cover the ordinary, as distinct from war, expenditure of the Reich. To be sure, taxation alone could not have paid for the war — none of the belligerents adopted this method. In Britain only one third of the war expenditure was paid for by taxation. If Germany had resorted to taxation, in preference to the issue of war bonds, for the purpose of skimming off purchasing power, at least the inflationary effect of interest payments would have been avoided. Drastic taxation would also have had important psychological and political consequences in the short as well as the long term. In the first place, by taking away excessive war profits it would have created the impression that all classes were making an equal sacrifice on behalf of the war effort, and therefore mitigated the resentment against those who had benefited from the inflationary boom, a resentment that was carried over with such dire results into the post-war inflation. In the second place, and perhaps with even more importance in view of later developments, keeping the early Inflation under strict control and nipping it, so to speak, in the bud would have prevented that toleration and lax acceptance, even enjoyment of inflation that was inherited by post-war Germany and stifled its willingness to resist.

Germany ended the First World War in the grip of an inflation of considerable dimensions. The currency in circulation was several times what it had been before the war; the floating debt of the Reich, reckoned in hundreds of millions before the war, had risen to many thousands of millions; there were many more thousands of millions in war loans in the hands of the public, and these, when sold, would create more purchasing power and inflationary pressure. As a result, the value of the mark, by the end of the war, had dropped in the international exchange markets: the pre-war rate of 4·20 marks to the dollar had risen to 6·60, and reached 8·57 in January 1919. Prices inside Germany had roughly doubled. Yet the German people remained unaware that their currency had been undermined and eroded. Indeed, it took them a long time to realise the meaning of inflation, and they blamed shortages of goods, the Allied blockade and so forth for the high level of prices. Foreign exchange rates in the blockaded Germany of wartime, the "Fortress" Germany, were not a matter of common knowledge or interest. Naturally everybody grumbled about the high cost of living and rising prices; but then, with the prices of rationed goods (and rationing, though diminishing, went on for several years) kept artificially low, and the prices for black-market supplies sky high, the very meaning of prices and their relationship to the value of the currency remained blurred. Besides, many people — shopkeepers and farmers, all those with an elastic conscience, and workers in the armament industry — earned well and spent freely. In addition, there were the big business and industry concerns and the *Raffkes*, the genuine war profiteers.

When, on 11th November 1918, Germany signed the armistice in the Forest of Compiègne, the country and its economy were utterly exhausted. The population was weakened by the great blood-letting, the exertions and the near-famine of the war years. There were about 6 million war casualties, counting dead and wounded, and the mortality rate of the civil population had also risen considerably in consequence of the war. Thus productivity had diminished and the reserves of food and raw materials were depleted; and in the same period the German word *Ersatz* began to acquire its meaning of shoddy and inadequate substitutes for desperately scarce goods.

Industry had largely been converted to the production of the necessities of war and was unable, without further investment, fully to supply the long-unsatisfied needs of the population. The machinery of the State had become rusty, inefficient and expensive to run. The transport system was in disarray and worn out after the extravagant use of it for military purposes, and the situation was aggravated by the conditions of the armistice, which, apart from the surrender of huge quantities of war material, imposed on the Germans an obligation to deliver 5,000 railway engines, 150,000 railway wagons and 5,000 lorries.

Money was needed to try and make up all these deficiencies, and to set the ailing home economy in motion — an expensive business, with productivity as low as it was. Likewise, money was needed to buy food and raw materials from abroad, and this meant foreign currency.

Further burdens were to come with the signing of the Treaty of Versailles on 28th June 1919. This deprived Germany of some 13 per cent of its pre-war territory, including many rich industrial, mineral and agricultural resources, and this loss of its former riches correspondingly reduced the country's capacity to face the financial difficulties generated by the lost war.

Last but not least, the clause in the Treaty — Article 231 — whereby Germany had to acknowledge its guilt for the war imposed on it an obligation to compensate the Allies for the damage they had suffered in consequence of the war. Deliveries in kind, which would be computed in the final amount of reparation payments, to be established at a later date, had to be made immediately.

Meanwhile, the legacy of the war had to be liquidated by the men who had taken on the frightful task of steering the young Republic that had emerged after the defeat and collapse of the Kaiser's Germany. They had to do it in a climate of near-anarchy. In many parts of Germany the workers went on strike and resorted to violence in order to defend what they thought were the achievements of their revolution: the replacement of the old monarchist régime by a social, democratic and progressive state. There was a communist insurrection in Berlin; a Soviet republic was proclaimed in Bavaria; there were workers' uprisings in Bremen, Hamburg, Halle, Brunswick, Thuringia and the Ruhr. The government, weak as it was, had to call upon the help of the military and the so-called "Free Corps", mostly monarchist and radical right-wing organisations of fighting men, who not only bloodily suppressed the hated forces of the Left, but also asserted their own power, thus impairing the authority of the republican leaders.

In these appalling circumstances Germany's new rulers had to find the means to replenish the country's inadequate stocks of food, raw materials — in short, everything that was needed to keep it going. At long last the wartime blockade was lifted, and by the end of March 1919 imports began to reach Germany — but they had to be paid for. The demobilisation of the armed forces was an extremely costly business, and so too was unemployment caused by the return of the soldiers and the redeployment of industry. War victims had to be cared for, pensions had to be paid. The new democratic government had to show that it had a social conscience even at the risk of incurring blame for being extravagant. But at the same time it did not feel strong enough to resort to drastic fiscal measures to cover, in part at least, the huge expenditure: revealing to the nation the full extent of its plight would have meant jeopardising what popularity it had and thus inviting disaster. Germany's obligations under the terms of the armistice and Treaty of Versailles lent weight to the argument that, so long as that drain on its resources continued, it would be hopeless to put the finances of the State on a more solid basis.

Thus it was decided that the bulk of government expenditure would continue to be covered by borrowing, deficit spending, printing more money, and inflation — in short by the depreciation of the currency. A few figures tell the story. Between November 1918 and July 1919 (that is, after the terms of the Treaty of Versailles had become known) the deficit increased by about 50 per cent, the note circulation marched more or less in step, the dollar rate doubled, and internal prices advanced rather less, by 42 per cent. The dollar was then worth 14 marks.

The Great Inflation

It was fortunate for Germany that in that period foreigners were still willing to buy the paper marks that the Reich printed in order to pay for its large purchases abroad; they still had confidence in Germany and its economy. But, should that confidence wane, the accumulation of paper marks would be a time-bomb ready to explode the value of the mark.

In July 1919 the picture changed, and the value of the mark, in terms of the dollar, fell rapidly, the fall gathering momentum until, in February 1920, the exchange rate against the dollar reached 100 marks, nearly 25 times its pre-war parity.

The cost of living index, then published for the first time by the German Statistical Office, was 8·47 as against 1 before the war. To be sure, it was much lower than the dollar index; but, now that life had become 8½ times as expensive as before the war, some people, though by no means the bulk of the population, began to see things the other way round. It was the internal value of the mark that had diminished; the currency had depreciated.

In the six months up to February 1920 the note circulation had increased only fractionally, and it was therefore not the money supply that had caused the sudden drop in the value of the mark, but evidently the political factor of the Treaty of Versailles. The reparation figure, as we have said, was not fixed in the Treaty: it was left to a Reparations Commission charged to determine the definite amount by 1st May 1921; and, although some deliveries in kind started as early as August 1919 — that is to say, before the Treaty came into force in January 1920 — it was not until the spring of 1921 that cash payments for reparations assumed really large proportions. Thus, in a material sense, the German

14

economy was for the time being not dramatically affected by the actual conditions of the Treaty.

But international exchange markets are influenced not only by facts, but also by the anticipation of facts, and by confidence, or lack of it, in a country's future economic outlook. In addition to the reparations — an unspecified, and thus all the more frightening, element — and other economic provisions, the Treaty included a number of grave territorial clauses, which reduced the land area of Germany and envisaged in particular the loss of agricultural regions in the east German provinces of Posen and East and West Prussia, and the food resources they provided; also, in the south-east, of the valuable mining and industrial basin of Upper Silesia, second in importance only to the Ruhr.

These prospects of material losses, of instability, insecurity and confusion, aggravated by the humiliating war-guilt clause of Article 231, constituted a severe psychological trauma for the German people. It was an alarm signal for the whole world.

After the signing of the Treaty of Versailles, a certain degree of economic recovery took place in Germany. With increasing imports, food and raw-material shortages were alleviated, exports rose and production improved. Yet, in spite of all this, people were seized by a spirit of *sauve qui peut*. For example, inhabitants of the territories scheduled for cession, fearing that they would be forced to leave their homes and possessions, converted as much as possible of their fortunes into easily transportable assets such as gold or diamonds, and tried to transfer their moneys to some secure haven abroad. It was the beginning of a phenomenon that was to become typical of the great German Inflation: the flight from the mark into *Sachwerte* (real values) and foreign currencies, and the flight of capital from Germany.

To begin with, the flight of capital from Germany was prompted not so much by the little-understood erosion of the currency but by a more immediate motive: evasion of the high taxation that was expected to be introduced in order to cover high government expenditure. The demand for foreign currency that this stimulated, to the detriment of the exchange rate of the mark, subsequently increased enormously as the desire to get rid of depreciating marks gradually became more widespread; and foreign holders of marks, who realised that they had burnt their fingers by dealing in them, sought to change them into dollars. *Devisen* and *Valuta*, meaning foreign currency, were to become household words in all sections of German society. The dollar was regarded as the best currency, and before long the exchange rate against the dollar was being published daily in the press, information of great importance for the ordinary citizen, who could thus tell at a glance what the paper mark in his pocket was really worth. Thus, the dollar was elevated to the dignity of a yardstick for the value of money, a rôle it was to play for many years.

Currency and import controls were not of much avail. Consciences had become elastic, and they were helped for the time being by what was known as "the hole in the West". This was the picturesque description given to the fact that the occupation of Germany's western provinces by the Allies made effective customs and currency controls practically impossible, and through this gap money flowed out unhindered and goods flowed in, many of them not really necessary but considered by the buyer better than depreciating paper money.

The outflow of money from Germany and its conversion into foreign currency naturally depressed the exchange rate of the mark, and the expectation that it would continue to drop accelerated the process. The mark seemed doomed to a continual downward slide. Yet in March 1920 a dramatic change occurred: the value of the dollar, which in the preceding month had risen to about 100 marks, fell sharply to reach a low point of about 40 marks during the summer. It rose again, dropped a little, but for more than a year remained below its February parity. The mark was, broadly speaking, stable.

Various factors had contributed to this improvement. On the political scene, there was the failure of the "Kapp putsch", led by the radical nationalist Wolfgang Kapp. This was an attempt by the forces of the Right to seize power. The rising collapsed speedily, thanks largely to the strike action of the loyal working class; this gesture of support established a fair measure of confidence in the stability of the young Republic. At the same time, "the hole in the West" was closed by agreement between the Allies and the Germans, so blocking one channel through which unwanted marks had been flowing. Furthermore, during this period the Reparations Commission remained relatively inactive; the reparations problem, which periodically troubled the exchange markets, seemed to have lost some of its urgency.

Steps were taken to bring the finances of Germany into better order, by the reform (under the inspired guidance of the then Minister of Finance, Matthias Erzberger) of fiscal legislation. Besides its effect on such areas of taxation as the turnover tax, estate duties, and so on, the reform produced the outstanding "Reich Emergency Levy", with charges of up to 65 per cent on property values. The tax system and its organisation were well designed, especially as regards the Emergency Levy.

Indeed, after the stabilisation of the mark, one of Erzberger's successors in his ministerial office paid tribute to his creation, without which, it was said, stabilisation would not have been successful.

However, in the political and economic climate of the earlier days, it failed substantially to consolidate the troubled finances of the Reich. The new machinery instituted by the tax reform was untried and slow, and, after the spell of stability in 1920–21, could not keep pace with the mounting inflation; taxes, when paid, yielded in real value only a fraction of what they were meant to. The opposition of the property-owning classes of the Right was reinforced by their hatred of the initiator of the reform, Erzberger, the man who had conducted the armistice negotiations and stood for reconciliation with the Allies. He became the target of a vicious vilification campaign, had to resign, and finally fell victim to political assassins. His enemies combined their hostility to the man with an inclination to sabotage his work, and tax evasion and the flight of capital received an added stimulus as a result.

Nevertheless, the initial impetus of the new tax laws resulted in considerable increases in the Reich's income: between April 1920 and March 1921 the monthly rate rose ninefold. Although the note circulation increased substantially, this was not accompanied by a commensurate depreciation of the currency, because confidence in the future of Germany and its money had returned: at least some of the new paper marks were taken up by foreigners, and, inside the country, those Germans who had been able to hoard foreign currencies sold them to the Reichsbank. This demand for the mark could not fail to support its exchange rate. Fortunately for Germany, prices of goods in the world markets now dropped sharply, thus reducing the country's import bill and need for foreign currencies. The near-panic following upon the signing of the Treaty of Versailles had calmed down; the external value of the mark had risen.

The German government has been widely blamed for not having made better use of this period of tranquillity to put the temporary stability of the currency on a more solid basis by stopping the policy of deficit spending once and for all — to defuse the potential time-bomb of the growing deficit. Whether the government lacked the power and ability or the good will to do so, it must have had another reason for hesitating to resort to deflationary measures. It is true that the mark could now look the dollar in the face; its external value had improved to such an extent that the gap between it and its internal value had narrowed. That was very pleasant for German tourists, who, for the first time since the war, were able to go abroad and to afford prices that were not so much higher than at home. But this seemingly golden era of mark stability had another side: Germany, having lost the price advantage over foreign competitors, found that exporting had become much more difficult; indeed, exports between May and December 1920 dropped by about 40 per cent, and unemployment climbed from 1·9 per cent in March to 6 per cent in July 1920, dropping only very slowly after that. Inflation seemed to have its advantages.

From June to November 1921 the mark fell again at an accelerating rate. It lost in that space of time about three-quarters of its value. The dollar rate rose from 70 to 270 marks; it was a foretaste of worse things to come.

Up to the time of this dramatic development, the reparations clause of the Treaty of Versailles had not yet been translated into concrete final figures. This posed, of course, a grave threat, but the very fact that it was vague still left room for a certain amount of hope, perhaps complacency. Now this situation changed.

Early in 1921, the machinery for fixing the sums Germany would have to pay as reparations had slowly begun to move. A conference held in Paris by the Allies arrived, after long negotiations, at a compromise according to which Germany was to pay the reparations in annual amounts of between 2 and 6 milliard gold marks per year, spread over a period of 42 years, and controls were to safeguard these payments. It was in this context that Mr Lloyd George took the opportunity of harshly criticising the Reich's fiscal policies, whereby the German people bore a financial burden ridiculously low in comparison with that of the people of the victorious Allies.

The German government rejected the Allies' demands, and the whole reparations problem was again thrashed out, this time with the participation of the Germans at an international conference in London. There was no agreement, and the German delegation, having refused to comply with the Allies' demands, were given a hero's welcome on their return to Berlin. The Allies replied to the German rejection by applying sanctions and occupying three German cities — Düsseldorf, Duisburg and Ruhrort — in the Rhine-Ruhr area. Any prospect of an agreed solution to the reparations problem had vanished. Some of Germany's leading personalities propounded the so-called "policy of fulfilment", whereby Germany should show her good will and try to gain that of the Allies by complying, as far as possible, with their demands; but this policy of reconciliation seemed to lead nowhere.

On 5th May 1921, Mr Lloyd George handed over to the

German Ambassador in London the final demands of the Allies in concrete terms — the famous "London Ultimatum". The total sum of reparations (132 milliard gold marks) was to be paid in regular annual instalments of 2 milliard gold marks, plus 26 per cent of the value of Germany's exports. A down-payment of 1 milliard gold marks was to be made before the end of August. There were the usual provisions of controls to guarantee these payments, and, as a sanction, the occupation of the Ruhr was threatened in case of non-acceptance.

The German government in office refused to accept and resigned. Hurriedly a new government was formed, and this accepted the ultimatum with the approval of the majority of the Reichstag.

The down-payment of 1 milliard gold marks due in August was made as stipulated. The acquisition of foreign currency for it — a highly complicated operation, with the international banking world supplementing the Reichsbank's own resources — would in itself have driven up the price of foreign currencies in relation to the mark. This natural and foreseeable course was aggravated when one of the international loans contracted by the Reichsbank — 270 million gold marks from a Dutch banking consortium — had to be repaid at comparatively short notice. Foreign currency earned by ordinary trade transactions was not available, and so the Germans had to purchase it by the sale of paper marks abroad — the paper marks being created by the discount of Treasury bills. The sale triggered off a vast speculative movement against the mark, which seemed to be well on the way down, and the anticipation of further falls encouraged speculators to accelerate their sales of marks. Whether, as was asserted at the time, these speculations were politically motivated, and originated by opponents of the

The Great Inflation

German government and its compliance with the London Ultimatum, in order to demonstrate that any payment of reparations was fatal for the mark, the lack of confidence in the economic health of Germany was real enough.

The situation was made worse on 20th October 1921, when the Council of the League of Nations decided that Upper Silesia should be partitioned and its richest industrial area detached from Germany and ceded to Poland. In accordance with the Treaty of Versailles, a plebiscite had taken place in Upper Silesia in March 1921; in this an overall majority of the local population had opted for Germany. When, subsequently, an uprising of Polish partisans was defeated by German, mainly irregular, forces, Germany's hopes of retaining that rich province were high. However, the League's decision dashed these hopes, and the ensuing gloom and despondency reached panic dimensions. It was one of those psychological shocks that resulted in the flight of capital out of Germany and the flight from paper marks to *Sachwerte*, thus influencing the fate of the currency. On 29th November 1921 the mark dropped sharply; the rate against the dollar reached 276 marks, having topped 300 earlier in the month. On 15th November, a further instalment of 500 million gold marks, due under the London Ultimatum, was paid. But the German government's protests that the country was unable to pay led to negotiations; cash payments under the Ultimatum were then reduced, and in August 1922, finally suspended.

The speculation against it having been overdone, the mark recovered, and on 1st December 1921 the price of the dollar fell to 190 marks. For three months the mark remained fairly stable at a dollar rate of around 200, but in March 1922 it resumed its downward trend, falling again to 270 marks to the dollar and fluctuating around this level until June. The currency circulation rose from 120 milliards in February to 180 milliards in June, the cost of living index from 24 (as against 1 in 1913) to 41.

In 1922 money had become very tight. Commerce, industry and agriculture all demanded credits that the banks were unable to give, and the Reichsbank thought it was its duty to provide the economy with all the means of payment it needed. The credit policy of the Reichsbank became increasingly liberal and it deliberately encouraged the greater use of commercial bills, which the bank, as promised, readily discounted, using the printing press to create the money needed for the purpose. In the course of 1922, the amount of commercial bills taken up by the bank rose from 1 milliard to no less than 422·2 milliard marks' worth. Commercial bills had joined the Treasury bills in their rôle as creators of money. In June 1922, the value of the mark began to fall again and fell faster and faster. So much did it depreciate, that the dollar, which in June had cost around 300 marks, cost about 8,000 by the end of the year. Indeed, the German Inflation had entered a new phase. Previously the depreciation of the currency had been a comparatively mild decline, the value of one mark although hardly more than one pre-war pfennig, still being considered as something real. This idea was supported by the intermittent upward movements in the value of the mark, for which these seemed to presage some kind of stability. The "flight into *Sachwerte*" and the flight of capital out of Germany had been confined to limited groups of people and had been prompted as much by the wish to evade tax as by the expectation of unbridled depreciation.

Now it became clear to all that the mark was galloping downhill towards an abyss. Confidence in the mark began to vanish and to be replaced by a widespread obsession about making the most of the inflation. There was profit in speculating on the further fall of the mark, and everybody clever enough to do so tried to take advantage of the situation, spending the elusive gains in wild sprees. If money was dying, it was just as well to have some fun before the funeral . . .

A number of events had prepared the ground for this development. At the international conference in Cannes in January 1922, there seemed to develop — at first under the auspices of Mr Lloyd George and the French Prime Minister, M. Aristide Briand — a climate more favourable to Germany, but this came to nothing when Briand suddenly resigned his office. He was succeeded by M. Raymond Poincaré who was, to put it mildly, much less benign than his predecessor in his attitude towards Germany. In the succeeding April, the conference at Genoa did not help towards the solution of the reparations problem.

Then, on 10th June 1922, the so-called Morgan Committee (presided over by the American banker J. Pierpont Morgan, and with a membership of Belgian, British, Dutch, French and German experts) reported, the French member, M. Sergent, dissenting. The committee had been asked by the Reparations Commission to investigate the possibilities of a foreign loan for Germany. Its conclusion was, briefly, that such a loan was unlikely to be obtained without a previous agreement on Germany's reparations debts and the stabilisation of the German currency. It seemed to support the German thesis that Germany could put its finances in order and stabilise the currency only after, at the least, a period of respite from its obligation to pay reparations. The French attitude obviously ruled out any implementation of the Committee's suggestions.

The climate of apprehension and pessimism thus created was enormously aggravated, and turned into despair, by the assassination of the German Foreign Minister, Walter Rathenau, by right-wing fanatics. This event, which took place on 24th June 1922, shook the country to its foundations. Hopes for the consolidation of the State, both internally and in its relations with the outside world, dropped abruptly.

For many Germans, Rathenau had been a symbol of hope for the democratic future of their country. A man of great ability, vision and intellectual power, he was almost unique among Germany's leading personalities in possessing at the same time the glamour badly needed to arouse any enthusiasm for the new Republic. In the Cabinet of Reich Chancellor, Joseph Wirth, which took office in May 1921, he had served as Minister of Reconstruction and, later, as Foreign Minister. He was one of the main exponents of the "policy of fulfilment", which had sought to solve the reparations problem by concessions and agreement. This policy seemed to have died with Rathenau. Any prospects of a permanent reconciliation with Germany's wartime enemies appeared to be utterly remote, while the danger from the enemy within loomed larger than ever.

The Rathenau murder and its repercussions had a direct and prompt effect on the course of the German Inflation; indeed, it can be considered as its turning point. Everybody living in Germany at the time felt this, and the view was supported even by a decision of the German Supreme Court, on 20th April 1926. Its shock effect turned inflation into runaway inflation. Ordinary people who had witnessed the rise in prices without having so far interpreted it correctly — as a depreciation of money —

now realised that it was the mark that had lost its value and was melting away in their pockets and bank accounts.

The mark, which before the murder had stood at 320 to the dollar, immediately sank to 353, and before the end of the month to 538, which meant that for the first time one mark was worth less than one pre-war pfennig. In August the mark plunged to 1,426 to the dollar and so it went on.

The day-to-day movement of the dollar became a matter of vital interest to everybody. The cost of living index shot up from 41 in June to 685 in December. The note circulation surpassed 1 billion marks and so did the Reich's deficit. For, owing to the delays in collecting tax payments and other revenues at a time when money was deteriorating rapidly, the real value of the State's income dwindled, covering only a small fraction of its expenditure. So the flight into *Sachwerte* accelerated and extended to the bulk of the population. All those who were able to obtain foreign currency bought and hoarded more and more of it and drove the dollar rate even higher. Attempts made by the government — through some 40 laws and decrees — to forbid the purchase of foreign currencies, or to compel those (exporters, for instance) who acquired foreign currency legitimately to sell it to the Reichsbank, had only very limited success. The authority of the State was almost as devalued as its money.

But it should be added that during the summer of 1922 there was full employment in Germany (over-full employment in today's terms), with the rate of unemployment remaining under 1 per cent from April to September and then rising only slowly, to reach 2·8 per cent by the end of the year. German industry, especially firms working for the export trade, was booming at a time when other countries suffered from economic stagnation. In the autumn of 1922 British coal-mines had their working week reduced to two days, whereas German miners did overtime. Indeed they had to, for the real wages of all workers went down disastrously: in October 1922 their earnings could buy only just half as much as before the war.

Yet, despite these sufferings, many people actually benefited from the erosion of money. There is the story of the compère in a Berlin music hall who used to address his audience "I see that many gentlemen in this hall are in high spirits tonight — it means that the dollar has risen again."

As the fateful year 1923 began, a dramatic development signalled the beginning of a new and more terrible phase of the Inflation, which would end, in November, with the complete collapse of the mark.

In January, French and Belgian troops occupied the industrial region of the Ruhr as a sanction for the Germans' failure to make certain deliveries in kind that had been promised under the modified conditions of the London Ultimatum. The deliveries that had not been made were actually a consignment of 125,000 telegraph poles and 12 per cent of the quantity of coal owed. Whether the French acted from ulterior motives in taking such drastic steps to assert their rights over what was a relatively small matter, or whether it was the Germans that did so by not making a special effort to avoid giving the French such a pretext, is a moot point. Whatever the rights and wrongs on either side, the whole German nation was outraged by the occupation and determined to make a stand against it. Workers and industrialists, and all political parties, ranging from the

Left to the extreme Right, were of the same mind.
Indeed, never since the outbreak of war had the nation
been so united behind its leaders. People were
encouraged by the sympathy shown to them all over the
world, even in the victorious countries, and prepared to
make sacrifices in their struggle. There were arrests,
bloodshed, loss of life.

But the fight was doomed to failure, because
economically it could not be sustained. Financed by the
printing press, it gave the *coup de grâce* to the mark;
and, when the mark had fallen from the rate of 18,000 to
the dollar at the beginning of January to 100 million in
September, Germany had to acknowledge defeat.

And this is how it happened.

The German government's reply to the occupation was
"passive resistance". It refused to pay any further
reparations and ordered a general stoppage of work of
civil servants and railway workers and a cessation of all
activities that might benefit the occupying powers. The
occupation forces succeeded only to a degree in restoring
production in the Ruhr ("You can't dig coal with
bayonets", the slogan went). But for Germany the results
were much worse. Not only did she lose the vast
productive resources of the Ruhr, and have to provide for
the unemployed and refugees who had lost their
livelihood because of the passive resistance; she also had
to cope with the damage caused to the rest of the country
by unemployment, dislocation, and administrative difficulties. One example of this will suffice: the German
railways, which to a great extent relied on the coal from
the Ruhr mines to supply their needs, suddenly found
themselves without these supplies and were obliged to
import coal from Britain in order to continue their
essential services. The operation meant a huge outlay of

foreign currency, to the great detriment of the exchange rate of the mark.

All this involved Germany in fantastic costs, which were almost entirely covered by the printing press. The note circulation increased from 1 billion marks at the end of 1922 to 92·8 trillion by 15th November 1923. According to the Reichsbank Report for 1923, it reached at the end of the year the staggering sum of 496·5 trillion, not to mention the so-called "emergency money", which added to the flood of paper another estimated 400 to 500 trillion. The floating debt on 15th November stood at 189 trillion marks. In those critical months only some 3 per cent of the Reich's expenditure was covered by taxes and other income; the rest came from the printing press.

In this final period of the Inflation, prices and the cost of living rose quickly, first closing the gap between lower internal and higher external prices and then reversing it. The flight into *Sachwerte*, the frantic urge to buy, combined with the reluctance of producers and owners of goods to sell for depreciating marks, naturally drove prices up. People in business down to the smallest shopkeeper had learned from experience that selling for depreciating marks made it impossible for them to replenish their stocks and involved them in real losses of capital. So they calculated or invoiced in gold or dollars on the basis of the "replacement" price of their wares, and for good measure augmented prices by "risk premium", which took into account the possibility of future depreciation.

The increased level of prices put an end to the inflationary boom Germany had been enjoying. The country was no longer fully competitive in world markets, in spite of the falling exchange rate. Only by dumping (that is, selling at a loss) was it possible to export at all.

The Great Inflation

Even the tourist trade suffered, as foreigners left the country where they were no longer able to live cheaply.

The high prices ultimately deterred buyers, yet did not diminish the reluctance of producers, especially food producers, to part with their goods. The complications of doing business in the money chaos led to stagnation of the economic life of the nation and lowered productivity, which in turn was mirrored in higher production costs and prices.

Production dropped steeply, and the rate of unemployment, negligible a year earlier, shot up from 6 per cent in August to 23 per cent in November. Unemployed workers were counted in millions.

The German economy was in a process of rapid disintegration, and inflation was pushed over the edge. The mark plunged down, not from month to month, or from week to week, but from day to day — indeed, hour to hour. On 13th November 1923 the dollar was quoted officially at 840 milliards, the day after at 1,260 milliards, after another 24 hours at 2,520 milliards, and, on 20th November, when the rate reached its maximum, at 4,200 milliards.

In these circumstances conditions of life became grotesque and unbearable, and as money was dying of this feverish disease, so were reason and common-sense.

Thousands of printing presses disgorged mountains of pieces of paper called "money", which were rushed by rail, road and air to desperately waiting crowds, hoping to get the stuff in time to buy the necessities of life before inflation had made it worthless. But, however quickly they grabbed the packets of marks thrown down to them, however quickly they ran to do their shopping, more often than not they were too late, as the dollar had jumped again while they were on their way. In the Berlin markets, the price of potatoes, eggs and butter were changed six times in one day. Grocers refused to part with their goods against paper money and barter trade widely replaced cash transactions. People had to offer their last pieces of jewellery and furniture in order to get their daily bread. Many had nothing to offer and there was widespread undernourishment and near-starvation. The angry and desperate masses became unruly and there were riots all over Germany. The Inflation had turned Germany into a gigantic madhouse, with the inmates dancing a St Vitus dance of the billions.

The whole German nation, including those who had drawn some (often illusory) advantage from the situation realised that this madness could not go on. Something had to be done. The disaster of the Ruhr episode had brought home to all that the past, with its endless convulsions, caused at least in part by the constant haggling over reparations, had to be liquidated and new initiatives taken. Dr Stresemann had become Chancellor in August 1923 and his aim was a policy of reconciliation, re-echoed on the Allied side, even in France. In this atmosphere it became possible to embark on the search for a solution to the problem of inflation. For this, the nation was crying out.

At long last, the plans to stabilise the currency, which had been under discussion for some time, ripened, and in November 1923 they reached maturity. With this the great German Inflation was, to all intents and purposes, over.

A complex of economic doctrines and political ideas translated into practical policies determined the course of the great German Inflation. The men identified with these ideas were statesmen, administrators, politicians, bankers, scholars — leading personalities in all walks of life. They were motivated by a variety of elements: past experience, tradition, dogma, and the national interest as they saw it from their diverse viewpoints, those of political passion, self-interest and personal gain.

The basic controversy about the root cause of the collapse of the German currency and the chances of preventing it hinged on the clash between two theories.

The upholders of the first theory (the exchange rate or balance of payments theory) sought the cause of the disaster in an outside factor. In their view, the passivity of the German balance of payments, begun during the war, continuing after it, and worsened to a considerable degree by the payment of reparations, produced a deterioration of the exchange rate, an increase of import and domestic prices and a decline in the internal value of the mark. This forced the government to relax its credit policies and to resort to deficit spending and the printing of more money.

The upholders of the second theory (the inflation theory, or theory of the creation of currency and credit) saw the sequence of events in exactly the opposite way. In their view, the circle started inside Germany with the Reich's deficit spending and the creation of more credit and money in circulation, and it was this that caused the decline of the mark.

In other words: did the deficit spending and the ensuing flood of paper money produce the depreciation of the mark or did the depreciation of the mark lead to deficit spending and the flood of paper money? And consequently: in order to end the chaos, was the first essential to stop the flood of paper *inside Germany* or to take action *outside Germany* — for instance, by obtaining a moratorium on reparations payments — in order to right the balance of payments and prop up the exchange rate of the mark?

Germany's official financial policy was dominated by the former, the balance of payments, theory. It saw in the passivity of the balance of payments and the deterioration of the mark in foreign exchange markets the factor that led to rising prices and inexorably forced Germany to create additional purchasing power by expanding credit and currency circulation by means of the printing press. Rudolf Havenstein, President of the Reichsbank, was the chief exponent of this opinion. For him, the issue of more money and the granting of credit facilities by the Reichsbank was simply an inevitable response to rising prices, a sacred duty to supply the economy with the means of payment without which it could not continue.

The City Treasurer of Frankfurt-am-Main, in charge of the issue of emergency money, summed up the gist of that doctrine in a more homely way: "I have printed the lot, everything — I print anything people demand." Years later, a Memorandum of the German Statistical Office concluded, "The fundamental cause of the dislocation of the German monetary system is the disequilibrium of the balance of payments. The disturbance of the national finances and the inflation are in their turn the consequences of the depreciation of the currency."

The persistence of the view that outside circumstances had forced Germany to resort to deficit spending and the printing of more and more paper money had important consequences. For the idea that the German currency disaster originated from causes outside the jurisdiction of those in charge of German financial policy crystallised around the problem of Germany's reparations debt. To what extent that was true, whether the argument is defeated by the simple fact that the decline of the mark started long before any reparations were paid and that indeed the mark was actually stabilised before the reparations problem was finally settled — all this is beside the point.

What is important is that Germany's financial leaders were obsessed by their theory and took up a fatalistic attitude. They could not be budged from the view that the Inflation could not be halted nor the mark stabilised without a moratorium on reparations payments coming *first*, and they were convinced that they were powerless to bring the finances of the Reich into order and to restrain the printing presses.

The policy of drift followed by German financial leaders is all the more remarkable since, according to some authoritative voices, Germany could have stabilised the mark in 1922 by making use of the existing gold reserve and taking drastic fiscal measures. Professor Bonn recalls that such a suggestion had the approval of the Chancellor then in office, but foundered on Havenstein's opposition.

Writing in 1926, a few years after the stabilisation of the mark, the former British Ambassador in Berlin, Viscount D'Abernon, saw the real causes of the collapse of the mark in:

> (a) inadequate appreciation of the danger involved in an ill-regulated issue of banknotes;
> (b) demands for reparations payments, involving forced public expenditure without regard to the effect of these payments on State finance.

However, Viscount D'Abernon emphasised that the

primary cause of the collapse was not reparations, but the inflationary methods of financing the war. The reparations payments, he felt, were an aggravating element, because, although the Reparations Commission made constant efforts to persuade the German government radically to reform its taxation and currency, it was never prepared to give the government a long-enough breathing space to make such a programme possible.

But if those responsible for Germany's financial policies were honestly convinced of the inevitability of inflation as long as the reparations problem was not solved, there were undoubtedly also some who, for reasons of their own, welcomed the continuation of inflation.

In the first place, inflation offered ammunition for the nationalist propaganda against the Allies and those German politicians who favoured a policy of accommodation with them. By pillorying these policies as responsible for the Inflation and the ruin of Germany, they had found a weapon against their adversaries at home and abroad. It seems fair to assume that this propaganda had some adverse effect on the course of the Inflation. For, on the one hand, it helped to discredit in every sense of the word the German democratic State, and, on the other, it strengthened the attitude of the Havensteins.

In the second place, many people drew large profits from the Inflation and the opportunities for speculation and other commercial gains it afforded, and therefore had a material interest in its continuation. Whatever the intentions of these men — and it has been suggested that for some of them the destruction of democratic Germany was at least a secondary motive — it seems certain that their operations not only resulted in profits for themselves, but actually contributed to the decline of the mark.

Finally, there was the argument that the Inflation and the depreciation of the mark were actually beneficial to the German economy by creating favourable conditions for the export trade, attracting foreign visitors and so helping the tourist trade, and also by stimulating domestic demand and production as a result of anticipation of further price increases. The representatives of German industry in particular never tired of propagating this thesis and warning against the dire consequences that a reversal of the downward trend of the mark would have for the export trade, employment and the German economy as a whole.

These Cassandra cries must certainly have sustained the German leaders in their reluctance to combat inflation drastically. Indeed, Germany hardly suffered from the economic depression that affected other countries in the early nineteen-twenties. But against this it has been pointed out that the prosperity engendered by the Inflation was imaginary rather than real. Not only did the adverse effects of the Inflation reach further and further into the nation, creating distress and a potentially explosive situation, but even those businessmen who apparently did well in selling their wares at inflationary prices to eager customers had ultimately to realise that their business was in fact a bargain sale with diminishing returns and a loss of substance. In the end, faced with total economic collapse, even the most enthusiastic advocates of inflation changed their minds.

If it is right to say that the origins of the great German Inflation were "made in Germany", it is also generally conceded that it was the reparations problem that aggravated it, made the stabilisation of the mark more difficult, and hastened the depreciation, if only because the recurring crises arising from the reparations problems encouraged reiterated bouts of speculation against the mark. It was a vicious circle which could be broken only by solution of the dilemma regarding which should come first: a moratorium on reparation payments or stabilisation of the mark.

There seemed to be a chance of reconciling the contrasting opinions and arriving at a compromise. Germany would break the vicious circle by stabilising the currency first, and by simultaneously showing her good will to the Allies she would create a climate in which there would be a reasonable probability of the Allies' granting a moratorium and fair terms for a reparations settlement. Professor Bonn suggested this possibility, and he writes in this context: "I was well aware of the risks of provisional stabilisation if it was not followed by a moratorium. But I was convinced that the Allied creditors would not dare to foil a successful experiment once Germany's good faith was proved."

Professor Bonn notes that later this thesis was indeed proved when the "miracle of the Rentenmark", the successful stabilisation of the mark in November 1923, was followed and reinforced shortly afterwards by the Dawes Plan. For this scheme, by taking the heat out of the reparations problem, provided the necessary breathing space during which the German economy and currency could achieve stability.

PART II

Chapter 1

A Licence
to Print Money

The most popular image of the great German Inflation, its symbol, is that flood of paper money which, issuing from the printing presses, engulfed the nation and the ship of state desperately trying to keep afloat. The struggle was hard, tragic, grotesque and often ridiculous, and innumerable stories are still told about it. In Pearl Buck's *How it Happens* . . . a German girl neatly sums it up: "You could see mail carriers on the streets with sacks on their backs, or pushing baby carriages before them loaded with paper money which would be devalued the next day. Life was madness, nightmare, desperation, chaos."

Curiously enough, what happened in the Germany of the nineteen-twenties was anticipated a century earlier in Goethe's *Faust*. The poet presents the devil Mephistopheles as the originator of the idea. The Emperor is short of cash so he complains to Mephistopheles:

Money is lacking — well then, create it!

41

The Great Inflation

and Mephistopheles accepts the task.

> I'll create what you want and more.

So the Emperor, in the interest of the common weal, of course, signs the prototype paper note which then

> . . . in one night was quickly multiplied a thousand
> times by magicians
> And so that everybody should have the benefit of the
> good deed
> We stamped at once the whole series:
> Ten, thirty, fifty, a hundred are ready.

And the Chancellor presents the piece of paper that has turned an ill into a good.

> To whom it shall concern —
> This piece of paper is worth a thousand crowns.

> (W. G.'s translation)

It is fitting that licence to print money should have originated with a spirit akin to the Devil, the father of lies. The currency of Germany during the Inflation years was a gigantic lie, which the nation recognised for what it was only in the last stage.

The road to inflation, like the road to hell, is paved with good intentions, and it was to turn "ill into good" that the German government gave the licence to print money. The object was to provide finance for the State's expenditure and to supply the means of payment needed by the economy.

The basic licences were given in the Financial Laws of August 1914, which included the institution of the loan banks; in the authorisation of the issue of emergency money (*Notgeld*); and in the relative toleration shown to the circulation of unauthorised emergency money.

In order to visualise what the end product of that licence to print money looked like, one must take into account the truly colossal amounts involved. From the the year before the outbreak of war, 1913, the total German currency in circulation grew as follows:

1913	6,000 millions
1914	8,703 millions
1915	10,050 millions
1916	12,315 millions
1917	18,458 millions
1918	33,106 millions
1919	50,173 millions
1920	81,628 millions
1921	122,963 millions

In 1922 it rose to 1,295 milliards, and, in October 1923, reached the sum of 2·5 *trillions*. By the middle of November 1923, it had risen to 92 trillions, and at the same time the total amount of all kinds of emergency money in circulation topped the figure of 500 trillions.

Before the 1914–18 war, the highest denomination banknote in circulation had been the 1,000 mark note, affectionately known from its colour as "the brown rag", and, being the equivalent of some 250 dollars, it was rarely seen by ordinary people. There were notes of smaller denominations, such as 10, 20, 50 and 100 marks, and these, together with gold coins worth 10 and 20 marks, and silver and copper coins, easily and quickly satisfied the population's cash requirements. Comparatively little use was made of the cheque as a means of payment, until both Government policy and public need increased the popularity of what were then known as "cash-less" modes of payment.

The years of "mild inflation" and correspondingly slow increase in currency circulation saw a change only in the sense that more of the same types of note were printed, including the loan-bank notes which came into use with the beginning of the war.

But that changed dramatically in 1922. As the note circulation grew, between January and December, from 115 milliards to over a billion marks, the official Reichsbank statistics show how large denominations came to the fore. Characteristically, the number of notes for 10, 20, 50 and 100 marks increased very little, but a new 500 mark note was first issued in August and the total sum in circulation rapidly increased between August and December, from 11 milliard marks to 133 milliard. The number of notes of the traditional 1,000 mark denomination increased in the course of the year from 53 milliards' to 584 milliards' worth.

In May 1922, 10,000 mark notes made their first appearance with a modest 19 millions' worth in circulation. This had jumped to 426 milliards' worth by the end of the year, when a new issue of 5,000 mark notes appeared — rather humbly beginning with 38 milliard marks' worth.

These innovations were authorised by a spate of government decrees and regulations aimed at meeting the mounting demand for means of payment which developed in the wake of the depreciation of the currency. The licence to print these mountains of money was there all right, but the difficulties in translating it into action and production led to muddle and all sorts of inconvenience for the public. For the first time since the crisis days of 1918, the State-owned printing house was unable to cope with the task and had to resort to the services of some private printers. Because of the need to simplify the printing process, a special decree of 21st September announced the issue of an *einfach ausgestatteten* (simply designed) 100 mark note. Soon afterwards a whole series of decrees had to authorise the introduction of eight different series of 1,000 mark notes, because of "difficulties encountered in the procurement of paper suitable for printing notes".

No wonder the public, already made nervous by the alarming pace of inflation, was bewildered and blindly accepted a rumour that out of the multitude of 1,000 mark notes in circulation only those bearing a red stamp were worth the full amount — giving them a sort of stable value. There was a run on these specimens and people hoarded them. The Reichsbank considered itself duty-bound to repeat previous warnings, and its official report carried the solemn words, "It should be emphasised that such notes do not represent a value in any way distinct from that of any other notes". The Report was presented on 30th May 1923, by which time the value of 1,000 marks was microscopic.

The story of the printed pieces of paper that went under the name of "money" was the same in 1923 as in 1922, with the sole difference that more and more noughts were added to the figures shown on the notes. When one of the largest banks in Berlin enlarged its offices by building two more storeys on top of the original, one of the directors, when asked why they needed all that space, quipped, "It will serve just to store all the noughts." The government printing presses could no longer keep pace. They were still printing 10,000 mark notes when the rate against the dollar had gone into millions of marks. Konrad Heiden, in his biography of Hitler, describes the nightmarish picture of a queue of people waiting in front of a shop with their bags full of paper notes. According to the figures inscribed on them the paper notes amounted to 700,000 or 500 million or 380 billion or 18 trillion marks. The people just lost count of their marks, as did even the Reichsbank. In its Report for 1922, the bank still carefully analysed how the notes got bigger and bigger and more and more numerous, and reproduced in detail the relevant regulations. In the 1923 Report such details were no longer given; instead, it was simply stated: "Keeping pace with the progressive depreciation of the means of payment in circulation, the devalued notes streamed back into the coffers of the Bank; again and again the currency circulation had to be replenished with new money tokens of larger denominations." So the 10,000 mark notes were quickly succeeded by notes for 50,000, 100,000, 200,000 marks; then 1, 2, 5, 10, 20, 50, 100, 500 million; 1, 5, 10, 20, 50, 100, 200, 500 milliard; 1, 5, 10 and 100 billion marks. Often they were hastily produced by stamping a higher value on notes of lower denominations, which, having become worthless by the time they were printed, had not been issued, but stored in the vaults of the bank. The largest denomination ever issued was indeed a 100 billion mark note.

To work in a bank in those days was a dizzying experience. Lisa Frank, a clerk in a branch of the Reichsbank at Rheydt, near Mönchengladbach, gave this account of it:

> Writing all those noughts made work much slower and I lost any feeling of relationship to the money I was handling so much of. It had no reality at all, it

was just paper. We had to sort so many different kinds of notes and count them. And if it didn't come out right we had to stay on at night and count and count again. It might be a million that was missing, but after all it was worth nothing. I also worked at paying-in department for cheques. If at the end of the day, your figures didn't balance up with the cashier's you had to find out where the mistake was, which meant checking all the entries with their enormous figures. Mistakes usually arose from transposing a couple of digits. There was a trick which usually worked in locating the mistake quickly. If you found that the last two figures of any sum entered was divisible by nine, that's where the mistake was.

A former member of a famous banking house in Frankfurt remembers the visit of an English uncle at this time:

Every morning our commissionaire went to the Reichsbank and fetched a quantity of banknotes, printed freshly overnight and neatly cut into blocks. A pile of this stuff was stacked in front of the cashier one morning when my uncle arrived. He took out a crumpled English five pound note. "Look here, my boy," he said to the cashier. "You know what this is? Now, will you tell me, if this is money how can that stuff be money; it looks quite different." He thought it impossible that those clean-cut blocks could be real. They looked like bricks, you know.

In fact the notes came so quickly from the presses that they were still damp when they reached the public and

47

sometimes the colour had run and the print was hardly legible. Often they stuck together, so people lost money that way, too. Sometimes they were deliberately glued together by cheeky youngsters, so that the numbers of noughts were increased and unsuspecting shopkeepers, dazed by the variety of shapes and sizes of notes, would accept them and give change.

Curiously enough, in the midst of all this turmoil, which required the cheapest and simplest methods of printing as much paper money as possible, the Reichsbank was still busy with the production of coins. A decree of 12th March 1923 authorised the minting of aluminium 200 mark coins, and another, of 8th May, the production of 500 mark pieces. In August 1923, over 24 milliard marks' worth of these coins were in existence (their real value at that time amounting to a mere 25,000 gold marks). Sensibly enough, a decree authorising the minting of aluminium coins for 1 million marks was never applied, and the existing coins of lower denominations ended up in the hands of scrap merchants. These minted marks were no more than a drop in the ocean of money.

It was the emergency money, however, that really swelled the flood decisively — by the colossal amount of several hundred trillions. Strictly speaking, not all the emergency money owed its existence to a licence to print it: some of it was authorised, some tolerated by the authorities more or less reluctantly, and some of it absolutely illegal.

It is a paradox that, with all the banknotes brought into circulation, "money was lacking" (to use the words of the Emperor in Goethe's *Faust*). There was not enough of it to supply the needs of the economy, to permit the payment of salaries and wages, and the purchase of goods and services. Indeed, that scarcity was the *Not* (need, emergency) that gave that money its name (*Notgeld*). The explanation for the shortage was simple: the real value of the money in circulation (as against its nominal value, which was rocketing) gradually dropped from 6 milliard gold marks before the war to some 100 million in November 1923.

The issue of emergency money, which had already occurred on a minor scale before that date, really got going in 1922. By that time it had become, in the words of the Reichsbank, "inevitable to have recourse to the issue of emergency money, in view of the sudden difficulties of providing the economy with paper currency". So an additional licence to print money of a sort was given by the law of 17th July 1922, which sanctioned the printing of emergency money with certain safeguards.

On an ever-increasing scale, public corporations, local authorities and similar bodies, but also private firms, made use of this licence to print money for their own financial requirements, and more than a thousand printing firms were busy manufacturing emergency money. In the end it was estimated that more than 2,000 kinds of emergency money were circulating, and many of them were not authorised. The whole thing became an absolute plague. The Reichsbank complained:

> Unfortunately, the regulations concerning the issue of emergency money were increasingly disregarded. In the autumn of 1923 the issue of emergency money assumed truly scandalous forms. Small and very small firms appeared as issuers of emergency money . . . without any scruples these issues were misused as a source of inflationary credit and profit.

The Great Inflation

Harold Fraser, a young English bank clerk working in Hamburg, reported on the state of affairs in Germany to his London office in regular dispatches. "There is still an alarming shortage of money," he wrote on 23rd August 1923. "Doubtless you have read that many firms have taken to printing their own notes. Many well-known concerns have done this and also the city of Hamburg Altona, the Railway and the big banks."

Indeed, what had begun as a means to satisfy a recognised economic need, namely to remedy the scarcity of ready cash, became sharp practice and a source of illicit gain thanks to the rapid depreciation of the notes once they had left the hands of the issuer. "The wild, illicit issue of emergency money beyond all economic need and for purely egotistic motives is one of the darkest phenomena of the grave inflation crisis" (Reichsbank Report for 1923). When, at the end of 1923, the German currency was in the process of being stabilised by the creation of the Rentenmark, Dr Schacht, the "father of the Rentenmark", recorded that the practice threatened to jeopardise the success of the whole operation. Some of the bodies that had indulged, very profitably, in the issue of such *ersatz* money, notably certain municipalities in the Ruhr district, had planned to finance a number of projects by printing more of it, regardless of the grave inflationary effect of such action. Only by forcefully restraining them could Dr Schacht frustrate this assault on the new-found stability. But not all motives were egotistical. Willy Derkow, a young student at the time, remembers how his uncle Karl, with a band of kindred spirits, set up a printing press deep in the woods. With this they produced "official" money and then, like modern Robin Hoods, distributed it in sackfuls to smallholders and peasants who had disposed of their land for money that had become useless, thus enabling them to buy it back.

But these notes also served some secondary purposes. For instance, many of them were produced with aesthetic considerations in mind. Many municipalities, reacting perhaps to the Reichsbank notes, which became more and more drab and dull, took pride in giving their money an attractive appearance by good design and the use of colour and witty texts — often in verse or in the local dialect. They advertised their local industries by the use of leather, linen or silk as the basic material. One town issued money consisting of leather suitable for soling shoes as a truly inflation-proof kind of currency. Even private business issued emergency money purporting to represent a "stable value". There was one firm that promised to the bearer of such a piece of paper "one pound of rye". Another one brought into circulation vouchers for "four packets of matches", with the added promise that those entitled to receive 100 packets could obtain them — packed in wooden boxes — ready for dispatch by the railway.

The towns and villages also indulged in a little political propaganda on their notes, particularly during the struggle against the occupation of the Ruhr, by printing anti-French slogans and caricatures on them. And of course they also had the collector in mind, although today the number of pieces of *Notgeld* in private hands is so colossal that it is difficult to believe that any collector is sitting on a fortune.

The problems and difficulties arising from the licence to print were enormous. They concerned the actual production of the paper money; its distribution to and reception by the ordinary people; and, in the end, the disposal of a mass of paper that had become valueless through the galloping depreciation of the mark.

The Reichsbank, cast in the unenviable rôle of provider of the wherewithal for the Inflation, did not acquit itself very well, as is proved by the inevitable recourse to emergency money. The President of the Reichsbank, Havenstein, declared on 25th August 1923, "The wholly extraordinary depreciation of the mark has naturally created a rapidly increasing demand for additional currency, which the Reichsbank had not always been able to satisfy fully."

Figures, in this wild dance of the billions, are all but meaningless and the cost of manufacturing banknotes, carefully entered in the Reichsbank Balance Sheet as

$$32,776,899,763,734,490,417 \text{ marks and 5 pfennig}$$

is a grotesque curiosity rather than a true measure of the effort. A more telling figure is that of the number of notes issued: a literally astronomical 10 milliards. A rough calculation shows that these pieces of paper stuck together end to end would form a strip capable of covering the distance between the earth and the moon more than three times!

The production difficulties were enormous. Already by 1922 the government printing works had had to expand their premises and organise work on a three-shift system, but since even this was not enough to satisfy the demand, 26 private firms were also printing money. Simpler techniques had to be applied to speed up the process, and the old copper-plate printing was abandoned and replaced by ordinary letter-press methods. Naturally, in 1923 the situation became more desperate still. Thirty paper mills were exclusively engaged in making the necessary paper, and twenty-nine firms supplied the 400,000 blocks required. The number of private printing firms working for the Reichsbank rose to 132. For these firms this peculiar licence to print money was good business, particularly welcome at a time when the Inflation was involving them in losses, for the Reichsbank paid in advance and thus assumed the depreciation risk.

One of these firms was the huge press and publishing concern of Ullstein of Berlin. In his memoirs one of the partners describes how one section of the printing plant was transformed.

> It did not print news but money. All the doors of the room were locked and Reichsbank officials were on guard. Round the machines were sitting elderly women, who stared fascinated at the machines from which the banknotes flowed. Their task was to see to it that these billion mark notes were put into the right baskets and handed to the officials.

Leopold Ullstein, a younger member of the family, still remembers that many of his maiden aunts were brought in to help and to see that the sheets were counted somehow.

The situation was aggravated when the printers went on strike for higher wages; that is, wages adjusted to the depreciation of the mark. One such strike, at the government printing works in summer 1922, had been the principal cause for calling in the help of private firms. In August 1923 Harold Fraser, in reporting that "there was absolutely no money to be had", gave as the reason the fact that "the printers in Berlin are on strike and so no notes are being issued". Many of the banks shut their doors to keep people out. Indeed, one observer sees in that printers' strike one of the decisive factors, the last straw, that made it imperative to stabilise the mark. The stopping of the printing press, even for only a few days, was sufficient to bring economic life to a complete standstill.

Having the masses of paper marks printed was one problem; handling them and bringing them into circulation was another. The "unprecedented swelling up of the business of the Reichsbank" manifested itself in the number of its employees, which grew in the year 1923 from 13,316 to 22,909. This was largely due to the complications in the handling, counting and distribution of the money. No fewer than 1,000 women were sitting in the despatch department of the Reichsbank doing nothing but checking the number of notes that came from the printing presses. These notes then had to be sent out to the banking institutions. In the good old days of monetary stability this operation had been carried out monthly; now, with mounting inflation and the rocketing demand for means of payment, it had to be done every day. Once upon a time, these parcels of money had been sent by mail; now, as the Reichsbank tells us, the size of the deliveries made it impossible to use the postal services, and the money, under the surveillance of the bank's own officials, had to be transported by rail, a single consignment often requiring several railway wagons. Numerous shipments left Berlin every day for the provinces. As the increasing rate of depreciation made it vital to deliver the goods with the utmost speed, some supplies were even sent by aeroplane, a form of transport rarely used in those early days.

If the Reichsbank more or less succeeded in the enormous and unproductive task of putting out the products of the printing presses, the problems that confronted the public at the receiving end were even more daunting. The problems were twofold: first, they had actually to get hold of the money, and, then, get rid of it, spending it in exchange for goods of any kind.

The scenes of people queueing up in front of banks and other offices in order to collect the money have often been described. Often, crowds of men would wait outside the branch offices of the Reichsbank throughout the night, equipped with boxes, baskets and cars, ready to receive a few hundredweights of paper money. Edith West was an English student at Heidelberg, in the fortunate position of having pound notes to change — if she could change them.

> There were always long queues at the banks. Sometimes before I reached the counter the window was shut. The supply of notes, which we were all waiting for and for which we had brought cases to carry them away, had run out. Perhaps the woman whose turn it was would let out a wail: "But what am I to do? There is no food in the house. The children are hungry!" "Sorry," the cashier might say, "but there *is* no more money." I, too, had to go hungry.

Harold Fraser reported, on 1st August 1923,

> There is now a great shortage of money and it is impossible to get more than the equivalent of £1 in any one day. This morning I was watching the huge crowd in the Deutsche Bank waiting to get money. There were so many people that queues approaching 50 people each were formed in front of each cashier. In fact it was found necessary to have policemen regulating the crowds.

And, on 23rd August,

> The banks in Hamburg are shutting their cash and

passbook departments on Tuesdays and Thursdays each week, and the consequence is that large queues are formed by 8 o'clock on the following mornings . . . lots of the smaller employers are unable to pay their employees who consequently go on strike.

One day during the height of the Inflation, Professor Bonn met a lady who begged of him,

Please give me something to eat. I am famished. I went to the country with a supply of dollar bills yesterday but the mark broke so rapidly that nobody could change one for me . . . I am waiting for the banks to open in the morning and hope that they have enough money to change a five dollar note . . .

The scarcity of means of payment manifested itself in a peculiar way in the shortage of notes of "smaller" denominations, say hundreds of millions, needed as small change for the really big notes. Thus, Hans Fallada (in his novel about the Inflation, *Wolf amongst Wolves*) tells the story of a cashier who had to pay wages to a number of workers. Handling money was becoming more and more difficult. He worked out the weekly wages exactly according to the wage scales — so many milliards and millions — but could not give them the cash.

There are not enough million and milliard notes, he has to take a large note, one of those lousy 100 or 200 milliard notes. He calls in four men: "Each of you touch one corner of the note — it belongs to you jointly . . . Now hurry off to town. Do your shopping together, you must come to an agreement." Well in the end they go out to make their purchases jointly. They find a shopkeeper who can change the note.

Konrad Heiden relates the typical case of a bank that, unwilling to keep alive an account with a credit of 68,000 marks, notified the customer that the account was closed: "Since we have no banknotes in small enough denominations at our disposal, we have rounded up the sum to 1 million marks. Enclosure: one 1 million mark bill."

One of the most pressing problems for trade and industry was the payment of wages, due both to the vast quantities of currency required and to the necessity for getting the money to their workers as quickly as possible, before its value could fall still further. Günther Porton-Seigne, an apprentice in a transport firm in Berlin at the time, relates,

> I remember vividly the pay-days at that time. I used to have to accompany the manager to the bank in an open six-seater Benz which we filled to the brim with bundles and bundles of million and milliard mark notes. We then drove back through the narrow streets quite unmolested. And when they got their wages, the workmen didn't even bother to count the number of notes in each bundle.

At one of the big electrical engineering companies in Berlin, pay-day, which had occurred monthly, came weekly, and later almost daily. Willy Derkow, the student mentioned earlier, was doing part-time work there:

> At eleven o'clock in the morning a siren sounded and everybody gathered in the factory forecourt where a five-ton lorry was drawn up loaded brimful with paper money. The chief cashier and his assistants climbed up on top. They read out names

57

and just threw out bundles of notes. As soon as you had caught one you made a dash for the nearest shop and bought just anything that was going. At noon every day the new value of the mark was announced and if by that time you hadn't converted your money into some *Sachwerte* you stood to lose a large proportion of your salary.

The money famine hit the smaller employers particularly hard. W. Bial's father owned a small brickworks in Gleiwitz in Silesia. He made his own arrangements for his staff.

My father began to pay wages largely in goods, mostly foodstuffs. My mother stacked these in the flat where we lived. Livestock, such as chickens, was kept in the bathroom and on the balcony. Flour, fats, etc. were bought in bulk as soon as money became available. My mother had to parcel all this food out in rough proportion to the employee's entitlement. Come pay-day, the work force assembled in the flat in groups for their handouts. In the early days of the inflation, my father had arranged for cows and sheep to be kept on grassy wasteland, and for some cereals to be planted, so some "home produced" food was included in the distribution. I still remember to this day, dimly, crowds of people in the room in the light of the lamps.

Another problem was caused by the racing printing presses: how to dispose of the notes that through the rapid depreciation had become absolutely valueless. There were of course those who framed them, or papered their walls with them or just put them away in the faint hope that they might in time become collectors' pieces. But that, of course, was neither here nor there. The real task was to destroy them completely and the Reichsbank went to it with all vigour. The sorcerer's apprentice had to get rid of the spirits he had called into existence.

The Salvation Army ran into problems with a collection taken up at one of their meetings.

> We had a clothes-basket full. The staff stayed up all night to count it, sort it and bundle it. We sent two boys off with it to the bank as soon as they opened in the morning but they wouldn't accept it. They said they didn't want all that stuff. The boys went to the post office and that was no good either. In desperation they made enquiries and found that the gasworks was obliged to take any kind of denomination so they took it there and exchanged it for up-to-date notes.

As these notes flooded back into the Reichsbank offices, the coffers were just not big enough to hold them even for short periods, and the regulations concerning their destruction had to be brought up to date. Permission was given to the local banks to send these notes to local establishments for repulping. Post offices got similar permission and finally special incineration plants were set up to burn the paper on the spot.

Money was dead and the corpse was sent to the crematorium for disposal.

Chapter 2

Prices and Incomes

William Guttmann was a student in Germany in the 1920s. "One fine day", he relates, "I dropped into a café to have a cup of coffee. As I went in I noted that the price was, say, 5,000 marks — just about what I had in my pocket. I sat down, read my paper, drank my coffee and spent altogether about one hour in the café, and then asked for the bill. The waiter duly presented me with the bill for 8,000 marks. 'Why 8,000 marks?' I asked. The mark had dropped in the meantime I was told. The 'index' based on the dollar exchange rate had altered so much that the price had gone up by 60 per cent while I was sitting at the table. So I gave the waiter all the money I had — and he was generous enough to leave it at that".

This is a typical occurrence of the Inflation and many people had similar experiences. The narrator in Pearl Buck's *How it Happens* . . . saw the price of a couple of rolls go up in the course of the lunch hour from 20 to 25 marks.

Business was no less affected in its daily dealings than private individuals buying their everyday needs. This is exemplified by a problem that confronted the publishing house of Ullstein in Berlin, one of the biggest of its kind in Germany. The sales prices printed on its magazines would be derisory by the time the magazines reached the bookstalls shortly afterwards, and how much more should the buyer be charged? On top of that, the baskets full of paper money brought in by newsvendors would have depreciated on arrival, to depreciate even more on the way from the publishers to the bank or the paper supplier, who would have raised his prices in the meantime.

Staggering though these price rises from day to day or from hour to hour were for the consumer, the movement of prices over the long term was even more prodigious, as the following table of examples makes clear.

Item quantity	Pre-war price	Price in summer 1923	Price in November 1923
1 kg rye bread	29 pfennig	1,200 marks (early summer)	428 milliard marks
1 egg	8 pfennig	5,000 marks	80 milliard marks
1 kg butter	2·70 marks	26,000 marks (June)	6,000 milliard marks
1 kg beef	1·75 marks	18,800 marks (June)	5,600 milliard marks

In addition, a pair of shoes cost 12 marks in 1913, over a million in summer 1923, and 32,000 milliards in November of that year. A newspaper then retailed at 200 milliards, and *one* match cost 900 million marks.

These figures, the number of digits a price tag showed at a given moment, are of course meaningless when seen in isolation. What was important at the time was the dynamic of the prices, their bewildering and quite unpredictable movements. These convulsions were not only responsible for changing the conditions of the German economy as a whole, but also for the uncertainties and complications besetting the lives of individuals. The struggle to cope with them led to social conflicts, general instability and much suffering.

The crux of the matter, one of the central facts of economic life in Germany from 1919 to 1923, was the disparity between the internal and external value of the mark. From the beginning of the Inflation until late summer 1923, the internal purchasing power of the mark was higher than its value in terms of foreign currencies or gold, and only in the closing weeks of the Inflation was this relationship reversed.

In practical terms that meant, for instance, that when the holder of dollars or pounds or other foreign currencies, changed his money in Germany into marks, he was able to buy more, to live better and more cheaply than he could in his own country. The exchange, as the saying goes, was in his favour. Conversely, foreign goods, priced in foreign currencies, were expensive for those who had to pay for them in German marks.

This phenomenon was expressed and quantified by two kinds of "index". The index of the external value of the mark was the dollar and gold index based on the pre-war parity of the mark of 4·20 marks to one dollar. That is to say that when, at a given moment, the exchange rate of the dollar was 420 marks (as it was in the middle of 1922) this index would be 100 — thus indicating the figure by which the paper mark had to be divided in order to obtain its equivalent in gold marks.

Let us assume that at the same time the cost of living inside Germany had risen — say, to 80 times what it was before the war. Then the index of the internal value of the mark would be 80 — the figure by which one had to divide paper mark prices in order to obtain their pre-war equivalent. The difference between the two indices would be the disparity between the internal and the external value of the mark.

The trouble was that this disparity varied very much

63

over the years of the Inflation, and it was this "dance of the parities" that kept life in Germany in a perpetual whirl. For just as nature abhors a vacuum, economic forces steadily worked towards filling the gap between the two indices, to adjust the internal value of the mark to its external value. But this process of adaptation was jumpy and erratic, in response to erratic and often precipitous movements of the mark in the international exchange markets. The exchange rate had become a shibboleth — and it may be mentioned in passing that in the current inflationary period of the nineteen-seventies a British minister accused the preceding Labour government of "having sacrificed the prosperity of the British people by treating the exchange rate as a shibboleth."

In recent years, the rate changes brought about by currency crises affecting the pound and the dollar, by the devaluation of these currencies or by the revaluation of the Deutschmark, have caused acute embarrassment to the tourist, who might suddenly find himself short of cash to meet his hotel bill. One can imagine the reactions of the Germans to the constantly falling value of their money, in the period of the great Inflation.

Through efforts to overcome the deleterious consequences of the depreciation of the currency, not only the price of goods but also the rates of pay, taxes, and so forth were kept in continual flux. The results were social tensions and widespread suffering.

Before gaining momentum, the adaptation of the internal value of the mark to its external value was slow and hesitant. This was due to several factors.

In the early days of the Inflation a psychological factor was important: as mentioned previously, it was generally assumed that the problem was not that money was losing its value, so making it necessary to spend it as quickly as possible, but that goods and services had genuinely become dearer. The public had not yet begun, as people used to an inflationary climate do, to *anticipate* that prices would rise automatically, thus making it advisable to buy today, rather than tomorrow, regardless of cost. Most people, therefore, reacted in the natural, traditional way. If things were too expensive they would do without them; they would buy margarine instead of butter, stewing beef instead of steak, one pair of stockings instead of two.

The experiences of W. G. illustrate how the situation affected people of limited financial acumen:

In April 1922, I went as a first-year student to Freiburg University, armed, as the son of an apparently well-to-do father, with a letter of credit for 10,000 marks, considered sufficient to keep me in funds for the four months of the summer term. The dollar rate then fluctuated around 300 marks so I would be able to spend some eight dollars, the equivalent of about 35 gold marks per month.

The price of a meal in a café traditionally frequented by students was then 18 marks (this is one of the few figures I remember with exactitude). Reckoning in gold marks, it was a fraction of its pre-war price, the 18 paper marks being worth some 25 gold pfennigs, whilst the pre-war price of the meal might have been one or two gold marks. But to me and a large number of my friends this seemed exorbitantly high, and so we regularly took our main meal in the Mensa Academica, where the price for an anything but appetising repast was six marks. The rest of our staple food consisted of coarse bread (then still rationed and low in price) with lard or a variety of cheese which was pungent enough to flavour the bread even if applied in minute quantities.

It was a steep descent from the standards of nutrition I had been accustomed to. I was permanently hungry, snatching every now and then a cheap piece of bread and a cup of *ersatz* coffee at the Mensa. Not for us the beer and wine and other small luxuries which had been part and parcel of a student's life in former days. Even the purchase of essential textbooks was reduced to a minimum. All this I considered just "too expensive" and I refused to spend my thousands of paper marks which were sitting, and depreciating, in the bank. Somebody cleverer than I, perhaps the bank itself or a borrower, must have had the benefit of my foolish misconception of the true nature of inflation.

But such naïvety was not entirely confined to those inexperienced in financial matters. Hans Fürstenberg has a story to tell about his father, Carl Fürstenberg, one of Germany's shrewdest bankers and well placed to cope with any financial problem. He too, in that early period, refused to understand the true nature of inflation and was convinced that the high cost of living obliged him to economise. So, to meet this high cost of living and to restrict his household expenses, he dismissed his cook. Even the expert of experts, Havenstein, President of the Reichsbank, shared such ideas for a long time if one can believe a story told about him. In 1922, it is reported, he remarked to a professor of economics that he needed a new suit, but, before ordering it, was waiting for the prevailing high prices to come down.

Because of this attitude and the economies people practised, demand slackened and consequently prices stopped rising so steeply. As a by-product, the money saved went into investment and improved productivity. This increased productivity had, in its turn, a mitigating influence on the tendency for prices to rise. In a peculiar way, this phenomenon extended even into a period of more rapid inflation in 1922, when there was widespread hoarding of money. In that instance the motive was probably more than anything else the speculative, if illusory, hope that the depreciation would be halted or even reversed. A German newspaper recorded in July 1922: "Because of the hoarding of great quantities of notes the internal depreciation of our currency was not completely shown in internal prices as compared with the external depreciation."

A more tangible cause of the relative upholding of the internal value of the mark was the damming of the price flood by government intervention. Indeed, the siege economy of the war years spilled over to some degree into the post-war period, in the form of price controls, subsidies and rationing for some essential goods, bread in particular. These controls were gradually dismantled, but bread rationing was not abolished until the autumn of 1923, and "free" and controlled prices existed side by side for many years, the latter giving the population a modicum of relief.

Transport, the mails and railway travel especially, was cheap. In fact it was ridiculously cheap, as, throughout the period of inflation, tariffs, calculated in gold marks, were considerably lower than they had been before the war. Indeed, for long periods they even worked out at less than ten per cent of the pre-war rates. Travel was therefore one of the few leisure activities that many Germans could still afford, and it became almost a mania. And whilst one certainly could not begrudge the hard-pressed population that pleasure, foreigners too benefited enormously from the absurdly cheap tickets, which they acquired with their own currency; in a similar way, foreign exporters made use of the low cost of freight, and trans-European transit trade was diverted to routes crossing Germany.

One narrator in Pearl Buck's *How it Happens* . . . refers to that puzzling phenomenon of low prices persisting in certain fields, and mentions, besides tram fares, the price of theatre tickets. Indeed, theatre and opera seats, admission to art galleries, museums, exhibitions and the like were very cheap; but these charges were often conditional on the presentation of a German passport, and foreigners had to pay more. On the other hand, the advantages foreigners enjoyed (such as first class travel on the railways, and meals at the best restaurants) fanned one of the nastiest by-products of the Inflation: xenophobia, the hostility towards foreigners reputed to be exploiting the distress of the German people.

Another factor keeping internal prices down, also a carry-over from the siege economy of war-time, was the anti-profiteering legislation. Heavy penalties, both fines and imprisonment, threatened what was called "usury": the sale of goods at exaggerated margins of profit, especially in the case of "chain-trading", when the merchandise passed through many hands, each middle-man adding his own profit. In a time of relative stability this legislation might have been appropriate, and fairly administered. With the progressive depreciation of the currency it became perverse, for it was dominated, for the greater part of the Inflation, by the principle "mark equals mark". This meant in practice that whether the profit was reasonable or "usurious", it was calculated by the difference between the purchase price, in paper marks, and the sale price, *also in paper marks*. Thus, if a shopkeeper had bought an article for 100 marks and sold it for 200, he was deemed to have made a profit of 100 per cent, whether or not the real value of the sale price of 200 marks, expressed in gold marks, would be sufficient to replace the article in his store. As, with the progressive depreciation of the currency, the shopkeeper inevitably, if he observed the letter of the law, made an actual loss on the transaction, the result for him was bound to be disastrous; stocks dwindled and could not be replaced and many law-abiding shopkeepers went to the wall. The black humour of the period produced the story of the nail merchant whose stock dwindled gradually to such an extent that ultimately he was left with just one nail — from which to hang himself. Indeed, prices were kept down as long as the rule lasted. But common-sense dictated that it could not last.

Of great consequence — economically, socially and politically — was the strict control of rents of private dwellings, combined with regulations about security of tenure. In a country where individual house-ownership was comparatively rare and the renting of flats widespread, this was of great importance. For many years rents were kept so low as to be negligible — in 1922 some two or three per cent of the pre-war rents, expressed in gold marks. Suffice it to say that by the end of 1922 rent constituted less than a half per cent of the average household expenses. If this was a blessing for the tenant, who was thus at least assured of a roof over his head, and a blessing for the employers of labour, who could successfully advance the lowness of rents as an argument against wage increase demands, it was a curse for the owners of blocks of flats, who saw themselves

69

deprived of the return from their investment in property, for the benefit of their tenants. This phenomenon and its implications will be examined in greater detail in a later chapter.

The matter was made even more intriguing by the fact that sub-letting — renting out furnished rooms — was not subject to the more severe restrictions applying to unfurnished flats. It meant salvation for many people who, except for one survival of their former affluence — their flat — had been rendered penniless by the ravages of the Inflation. This created the paradox that the tenants of the flats, who had invested nothing but their normal monthly rent, now absolutely infinitesimal, were making a fortune at the expense of the owner, who had probably sunk all his savings into the original purchase of the house.

The best catch for people able to rent out such furnished lettings was of course foreigners and others who were able to pay in foreign currency. In Heidelberg, Edith West paid her landlady in pounds sterling and got very favourable terms out of it for herself.

These "favourable terms" were, of course, only the result of the disparity between the purchasing power of the mark inside Germany and its exchange value. These terms, with the above-mentioned perpetual adaptation of the relationship between the two values, were not always so favourable, but at their best the low internal prices — low, that is to say, in relation to gold or foreign currencies — were staggering.

Many people still remember going on holiday to Germany to take advantage of the Inflation, and certain Germans, fortunate enough to possess gold or foreign currency, were able to do much the same in their own country.

Franz Schönberner tells the story of some friends who happened to find their late grandmother's discarded dentures with some gold fittings. With the proceeds they could afford to live in luxury for some weeks at a hotel in the Bavarian Alps. Similarly, a famous British economist remembers how, as a boy, he spent a protracted period in the best hotels of German spas: his father had decided that this was infinitely cheaper than living in England. Mrs E. Glücksmann tells of a week spent in a German sanatorium on the strength of a gift of £1. Mrs Albury claims that a week-end in Germany could be had for threepence, Mr Rosenthal got bed and breakfast for 50 French centimes.

These examples are obviously extremes, and concern periods when the dollar rate changed suddenly and internal prices took some time to adjust to it. But adjustment, with all that it implied for the instability of prices, always took place, sometimes slowly and sometimes more rapidly, until, in the turbulent year of 1923, adjustment not only became almost instantaneous but also overshot the dollar rate, so that internal prices actually became higher than international ones.

One of the problems posed by the modern inflation of the nineteen-seventies is how to allow, in company accounts and balance sheets, for the lowering of money values, and, thus, how to calculate true — as opposed to mere paper — profits. The oscillations of the true value of the mark during the great German Inflation magnified this problem and caused it to penetrate into all, even the most minute details, of the economy and everyday life. Something had to be done, for instance, to rescue shopkeepers who were losing their capital, as we have seen, by being forced to sell goods for less than their replacement cost, and to provide for a more effective system for adjusting taxes, railway fares and other tariffs.

Public opinion, for a long time mesmerised by the "mark equals mark" rule, and averse to the idea that the price of the dollar should directly influence the price of goods produced inside Germany, came slowly to realise that this was ruinous for the community as a whole, and the authorities followed suit.

From 1923 onwards, gold (in the form of pre-war prices), the dollar, or various other stable units were used, rather than the fickle paper mark, for the calculation of prices; "gold invoicing", as it was called, became almost universal in business.

Harold Fraser, in his dispatch of 6th October 1923, described what he saw happening:

> Everything is calculated in gold marks. For instance a suit costs 150 gold marks, and shoes from 20 to 30. If that is not done a *Grundzahl* (basic figure) is fixed of so many marks, and a multiplicator varying every day according to the dollar exchange is placed in the shop windows . . . This is in reality only a variation of the gold mark.

As time went on, the "multiplicator" (or "multiplier") would change twice a day, and the customer was like a dog chasing its own tail, as Edith West's story, related below, well illustrates. As an English student, she had foreign currency at her disposal, but she was caught up in the vicious circle like everyone else:

> I needed a coat, chose one, and went to the bank to fetch the money. When I got back the shop was closed — they closed for two hours or so at midday while the new multiplier was decided upon. The

price tickets on the goods were not changed. They remained at 18 or 20 or whatever it might be. But in the middle of the window was the multiplier. That day it was 50,000,000 — it had doubled during the lunch-hour — and when the shop opened the money I had drawn out was not enough to pay for the coat. And now the banks were shut again. Next morning the multiplier had gone up again. By the time I caught up, the coat cost a great deal more than I had intended.

The index, or multiplier, originally the product of a more complicated calculation than just the adopting of the dollar exchange, was, it was said, the principal axis around which all German life gyrated. However, the gyration was rather erratic, and did not produce entirely satisfactory results.

For instance, the multiplier for wages, generally based on the cost of living index issued by the Statistical Office, might not necessarily be the same as the index used by a shopkeeper. Moreover, there was often a time-lag, and the employee, having received his pay on the basis of the index in force in the morning, might discover that the shopkeeper, having perhaps closed his shop for lunch in expectation of a change, had in the meantime upped his prices. That was how the cost of W.G.'s cup of coffee and Edith West's coat jumped and brought the price of the goods beyond the money the customer had in his pocket. But shopkeepers were not much better off. If a shopkeeper sold in the morning at the index rate then prevailing, he would find in the afternoon that the index had by then doubled, thus halving the value of his takings, and he could buy that much less from the wholesaler. Attempts to anticipate such future alterations

73

were largely based on guesswork and were often more confusing than effective.

Though this adjustment of internal prices was merely realistic, bringing about the end of absurdly low real prices, its effect was to push prices not only up to international level, but even beyond that. This was a fact of the greatest importance for the development of economic conditions in Germany. Towards the end of 1922 internal prices averaged about 60 per cent of the level existing in the rest of the world; by autumn 1923 they had risen to some 110 per cent of that level.

What happened was that prices were calculated not only on the present depreciation of the mark, but also on the expectation of further depreciation, and for this risk a premium was added to the basic price. This rise lost to Germany one of the advantages it had derived from the Inflation: the edge over its foreign competitors, who enjoyed stable currencies. Exports dwindled, and those foreigners who had thronged Germany when it was a cheap place for them began to be deterred by the cost. (From 1922 to 1923 the number of foreign visitors to Hamburg, for instance, diminished by one third.) This was, in part at least, responsible for the slump in the German economy that led to high unemployment. On 6th October 1923 Harold Fraser wrote,

> With this tremendous rise in prices so is passing the time when Germany, owing to her bad exchange, could sell goods so much cheaper than other countries . . . This is well illustrated by coal. This commodity costs here in Hamburg for Ruhr coal 68 gold marks per ton, and for English coal only 31 gold marks. The difference is remarkable. At the same time the port of Hamburg which was able to

compete so successfully with London and Rotterdam and other places for the destination of goods, is now, owing to such high charges, losing a large amount of business.

And three weeks later he wrote,

Men are being discharged daily from the shipyards and factories, and the State pays a most miserable dole. Men, women and children in hundreds are on the verge of starvation and it is small wonder that shops are plundered, and that Bolshevism is gaining recruits every day. The prospect is alarming in the highest degree. Who is going to provide for an ever-increasing army of unemployed over the winter?

The inverse disparity — that is, the fall of the internal value of the mark below its exchange value — became staggering. It is best explained by the comparison of the *gold* prices of some goods before the war with those in November 1923: a kilogram of rye bread, worth 29 gold pfennigs before the war, cost the equivalent of 78 gold pfennigs in 1923; a kilogram of beef, which could be bought for 1·80 gold marks in 1913, by 1923 was costing the equivalent of eight gold marks; a pair of shoes, priced at 12 gold marks before the war cost 32 gold marks in 1923.

These price rises were erratic and convulsive and by no means uniform, but they put most goods out of the reach of many people and contributed decisively to the stagnation and near-collapse of the German economy. Shops remained empty, and their suppliers, unable for this reason to get rid of their wares, reduced production.

Dismissals of staff followed and provided more recruits to the steadily growing army of unemployed.

It is merely a commonplace to say that prices and incomes are closely linked economic factors. Unfortunately, they are not Siamese twins that develop and grow in harmony; and indeed, the ever-changing relationship between the two during the Inflation was a paramount fact of life with far-reaching consequences.

The depreciation of the mark exerted a direct and fundamental influence on two kinds of incomes: on the one hand, the fixed paper-mark incomes (and the fixed assets underlying them, mainly held by the middle classes), which the Inflation wiped out; on the other hand, the incomes (and resulting fortunes) that originated in the speculative exploitation of depreciation by inflation profiteers. These two categories of people, the typical losers and winners of the Inflation, are the subject of separate chapters. The incomes under consideration here are the earned incomes of workers and employees, and of the self-employed, including members of the professions.

By far the most numerous group among these was the working classes. The workers have been described as the main sufferers from the Inflation. This is a somewhat partisan point of view, but it is nevertheless true that they suffered considerably. Their standard of living was impaired and one phrase in a letter written by Harold Fraser on 27th October 1923 shows in a nutshell to what dimensions this suffering could go: "With a wage of 100 milliards, which is about the average paid this week, a man is faced with semi-starvation." But not all workers suffered all the time to such a degree; and if, in real terms, the average wages were lower than before the war,

The first instalment of the reparations payments made by Germany to the Allies.

Some of the currency in circulation at the height of the Inflation. The design and materials used became brighter and more extravagant, some being printed on leather and silk.

Walter Rathenau, Foreign Minister, whose assassination
in June 1922 precipitated the collapse of the mark.
(*Radio Times Hulton Picture Library*)

Rudolf Havenstein, President of the Reichsbank, whose
policies aided the development of the Inflation.
(*Radio Times Hulton Picture Library*)

Poster urging the Germans to boycott French and Belgian goods during the occupation of the Ruhr, 1923.

French troops entering Essen at the time of the occupation of the Ruhr, 1923.
(*Radio Times Hulton Picture Library*)

A cigar box replaces a pay packet (or a wallet) for a baker collecting his wages.

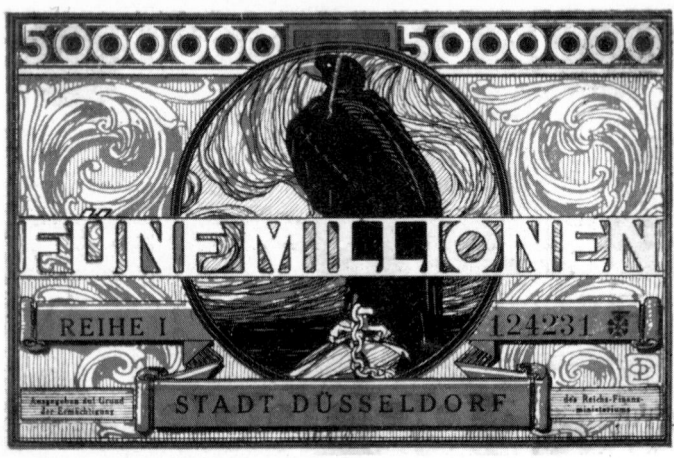

5000000 5000000
FÜNF MILLIONEN
REIHE I
124231
STADT DÜSSELDORF

A packing case serves as a till in a grocer's shop: the last sale on the cash register is a reminder of happier days!
(*Radio Times Hulton Picture Library*)

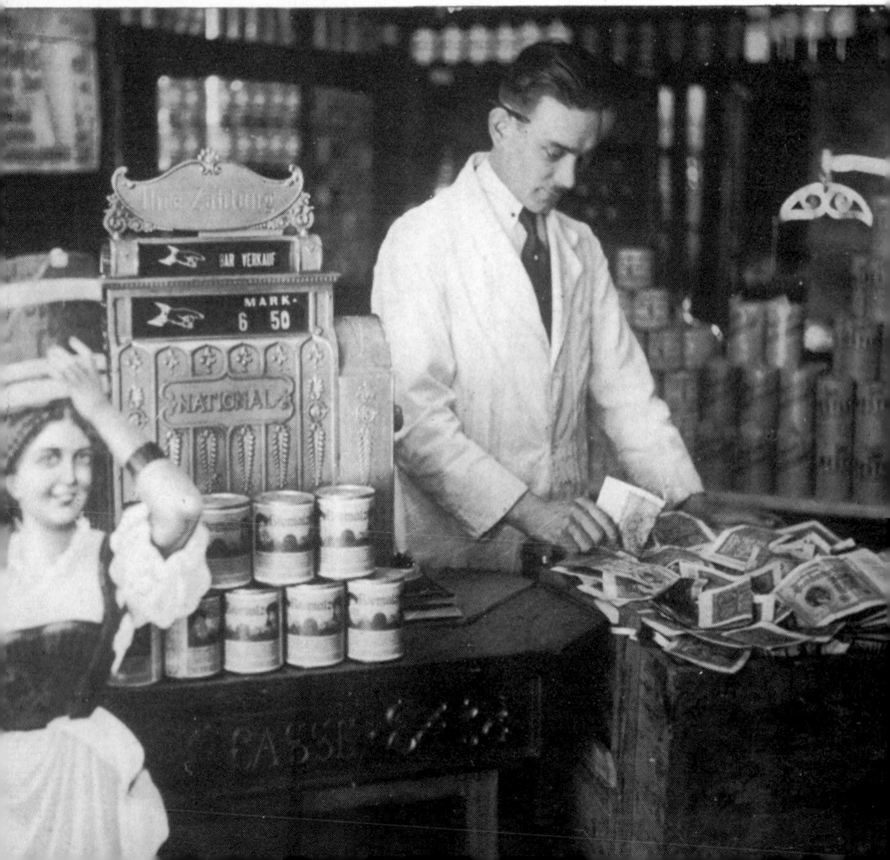
BAR VERKAUF
MARK
6 50
NATIONAL

B №018374 ✳

5 000 000 000

Deutsche Hansabank A.-G.
Filiale Alt- und Neuötting

Zahlen Sie gegen diesen Scheck aus unserem Guthaben nach Behebung
des Bargeldmangels an uns selbst oder Ueberbringer

Mark **Fünf Milliarden**

Deutsche Hansabank A.-G. Filiale Alt- u. Neuötting

Neuötting,
Altötting, 27. Okt. 1923

One of the "money shops", which were springing up everywhere,
announces that it is no longer worth giving change for the 10,000
mark note.

Waiting at the bank with large portmanteaux to make
withdrawals in the inflated paper money.
(*Bundesarchiv, Koblenz*)

"*Every day was pay-day*"—and only a furniture van was large
enough to deliver the wages to the office.
(*Bundesarchiv, Koblenz*)

this was to some extent compensated by the element of employment: as already noted, there were periods during the Inflation when German workers enjoyed full employment — at a time when unemployment was rampant in countries with stable money.

The working classes emerged from the 1918 revolution into the post-war period stronger than before. They were the pillars of the republican régime; their main representatives in the German parliament, the moderate Social Democrats, remained a very strong party until the Nazis erupted on to the scene in 1930. The workers were a force the State had to reckon with, and they improved their status in many respects. The position and power of trade unions, and the prevalence of collective bargaining, the eight-hour working day, and workers' representation on works' councils bore witness to this. The outcome was that real wages, which during the war had dropped considerably below the 1913 level, rose to such an extent that in 1919 the wages of skilled workers had nearly reached pre-war levels, while those of unskilled workers had risen far beyond them.

After 1919, the vagaries of the Inflation took over and monetary considerations determined decisively the level of both wages and employment. But even then the power of the workers was sufficient to enable them to exercise, both by persuasion and by use of the strike weapon, their influence on wages, especially in the last stages of the Inflation.

When the exchange rate of the mark dropped, prices rose, and so did wages. But, up to the end of 1922, wage increases tended to lag behind the upward movement of prices, with the result that real wages were reduced; and this process was reversed when the exchange rate of the mark improved.

The Great Inflation

Thus, at the beginning of 1920, the fall in the rate of the mark against the dollar in the ratio 100:50 caused the real wages of the miners to slide from 80 per cent to around 60 per cent of pre-war levels. Subsequently the mark improved, to reach what was, in fact, its best rate for the rest of the Inflation — around 40 marks to the dollar. Characteristically, this consolidation and near-stabilisation of the mark, which seriously reduced Germany's export trade and the country's prosperity in general, was accompanied by a considerable rise in the unemployment rate, which reached 6 per cent in July. However, for those who kept their jobs, real wages picked up again, in some cases reaching (in November 1921) a level as high as 97 per cent of the pre-war figure. The end of 1921 heralded a rapid acceleration of the Inflation, which was greatly speeded up in the summer of 1922 in the wake of the Rathenau murder, with the price of the dollar exceeding 1,000 marks in August 1922. This was reflected in an unprecedented drop in real wages, which at times were reduced to only half their pre-war level (47·7 per cent in January 1923). And although, as a rule, unemployment moved in harmony with real wages, sinking in mid-1922 to less than 1 per cent, and thus mitigating the plight of the working classes as a whole, for the individual worker in most industries the situation became desperate. Wages were, in many cases, below subsistence level. The working population was faced with starvation.

The pressure exerted by the trade unions and by the direct action of the workers in strikes and demonstrations was, though successful in obtaining higher nominal (paper-mark) wages, really of little avail as long as the "dance of the parities" continued and adjustments to the workers' pay limped behind the depreciation of the currency. By that time businessmen had already discovered that the only way of mitigating the ravages of inflation was to get away from the paper mark and to make their calculations based on a stable unit, such as the dollar or the gold mark. "We never thought in marks but in pounds," as a British businessman in the hides and skins business in Hamburg put it. In Pearl Buck's words, workers also

> . . . discovered the "trick of inflation" which was to figure the value of money in gold. What they asked for now was wages paid daily in exact accordance with the daily mark devaluation. Strike followed strike. The port, the workers' districts were seething with unrest. The closer the workers came to their goal the quicker the mark raced down.

The pressure exerted by the workers led to the introduction of various methods which were to guarantee that the money in their pay-packets would not be affected by the currency depreciation. The multiplier proved unsatisfactory because, between the fixing of the index and its application at the moment of payment, the depreciation had raced ahead, depleting the real value of the payment. Thus the multiplier came to be based on the dollar rate of the day, but by that time the speed of the depreciation was so great that the value of the pay packet sank in the time it took to cover the distance between the wages office and the shops. Spending one's wages became simply a race against time.

Lisa Frank remembers that, nearly every hour, a telegram announcing new salary rates used to arrive in the bank where she worked from head office in Berlin. The staff used to cash cheques and rush out to spend the money. "We used to have to sneak out one at a time because we weren't supposed to go out except at lunch time."

Dorothy Haenkel ran a Quaker relief depot beside a school in Frankfurt.

> Almost daily at the ten o'clock break I used to see the teachers trooping down into the playground where their friends or relatives were waiting, into whose hands they thrust the money that they'd just received so that it could be spent before the prices went up at noon.

One mother took her young daughter shopping with her just to do the sums; she couldn't attend to what she was buying and do the mental arithmetic at the same time.

Finally the multiplier was calculated on a basis of a prices forecast — that is, the prices the worker was expected to pay at the moment of purchase. This device was, so to speak, the mirror image of the already-mentioned method of adding to prices a premium to compensate the seller for further depreciation of the mark. These were highly complicated methods which not only caused confusion and a great deal of unproductive work, but did not really produce the desired result of overall justice and stability of the money the wage earners received.

Harold Fraser, regularly reporting home, was enjoying, as he said, "many interesting conversations with various people, from the Chief Director of the Deutsche Bank down to my landlady." On 14th June 1923 he wrote,

> Wages are supposed to rise in proportion to the rise

in the cost of living, but in reality this seldom happens. [But he remarks elsewhere in this letter that "All business here is conducted in foreign currency."]. . . The consequence is that the labouring classes are inclined to communism . . .

Yet, as he notes repeatedly, the workers were reluctant to revolt, and, although the communist elements naturally exploited the distressing situation for their political ends, the majority used their power only to fight for their livelihood and, their aims achieved, abstained from further agitation. "There are no strikes," Fraser wrote on 15th September, "in consequence, no doubt, of ever-increasing wages for the worker."

Indeed, thanks to the methods adopted for their calculation, the nominal wages in the last phase of the Inflation rose enormously, as did real wages.

But now, in the last months of the Inflation, the problem of wages was overshadowed by the spectre of unemployment. In part at least, this was the ironic result of the rise in wages. In fact, it was only one aspect of the distress and chaos that engulfed the German economy as the currency collapsed.

The lot of salary-earning employees did not differ very much from that of the wage earners, except for the fortunate few who had the chance of earning foreign currency. Robert Berman was paid in sterling by his bank. G. P. Henshell and his white-collar colleagues at the United States Consulate in Berlin were paid in dollars. The English exporter of hides in Hamburg paid his maids in sterling. Some people were paid in kind, or in the equivalent of a certain quantity of a commodity. Mrs Bayreuther's husband was a leather merchant in Tübingen: he did all his business on a dollar basis and they were well protected against inflation. They paid their maid not in money but in goods. At the end of the month Mrs Bayreuther would ask her, "What do you need — a dress, shoes?" and she would give them to her. Herbert Hochfeld found payment in kind particularly rewarding when he had to take work on a farm.

> Wages were paid by crediting me with a certain amount of rye every pay-day. Whenever I needed money I would go to the manager and "sell him" some of the rye standing to my account. Of course the price of rye was rising all the time so I could only gain by this system. My family thought that compared with others I was earning an enormous amount, but it was simply that I was always up-to-date with the cost of living, while others were not.

After he left the farm his good fortune continued, because he became an apprentice in a firm dealing with the import and export of cellulose in Hamburg and was paid in pounds sterling. Such people were the lucky ones.

As a pressure group, salary earners were probably less powerful than the organised workers, but they too gave vent to their discontent and struck for higher wages. By September 1923, Harold Fraser was reporting back to London,

> The people complaining most now are the bank clerks, many of whom are now conducting an over-time strike. The public suffer because all banks close down at 11 o'clock every morning and on Tuesday and Thursday are not open for cash business at all. In addition, amounts under M 50,000,000 are no longer dealt with.

But white-collar workers were unable to have their salaries adequately adjusted to the prevailing prices, and their real incomes were low. To some extent their plight, like that of the workers, was alleviated by their improved chances of employment. Here the impact of the Inflation and the conditions it brought about was direct. The enormous amount of administrative and paper work, necessitated by the constant variations of money values, the ever-changing calculations, the very counting and moving of the money itself, led to corresponding increases of staff in the offices and counting houses. The expansion in the office of the Reichsbank has already been mentioned, and this was typical of the great increase in the numbers of personnel all over the country.

Not all wages and salaries were uniformly affected by the Inflation. Indeed, the changes produced a sort of revolution in the incomes structure, a tendency towards equalisation of the earnings of such different strata as the skilled and the unskilled, the higher and lower qualified, the young and the old, men and women. The narrowing of differentials in these incomes was a by-product of the Inflation and it was of social as well as economic importance. For instance, the wages of unskilled workers, which before the war had been on average some 30 per cent below those of their skilled colleagues, reached, by 1923, almost the same level. Similarly, the differential between the salaries of higher qualified officials and the lower ranks narrowed during the Inflation years, so that, according to Professor Alfred Weber, such higher officials received in 1922 only about 25 per cent of the value of their pre-war earnings, while their lower-ranking colleagues received up to 82 per cent. The plight of the higher officials was aggravated by the fact that traditionally this group had had some private means, which helped them to maintain a standard of living commensurate with their social position; but, as we have seen, these private means had more often than not evaporated in the Inflation.

The fact that the vast mass of wage and salary earners received low real incomes was reflected in the general lowering of the standard of living — sometimes, as we have noted, below the subsistence minimum.

It is true that rent, one item in the family budget that, in pre-war days, had claimed a fair slice of the breadwinner's income, had disappeared from the household expenses almost completely as a result of the rent-control laws. But this was not sufficient compensation, and the German people as a whole became poor. The degree of poverty is impossible to assess exactly in statistical terms; but there are some indications.

Writing in 1923, Fritz Naphtali, a German writer on economics, refers to the struggle of wage and salary earners to adjust their incomes to the depreciation of the currency, and concludes that "the adjustment has succeeded to the extent that the income covers the current necessities of daily life. The impoverishment starts at the point where the problem of *Anschaffungen* [purchases of goods not for immediate consumption] arises." For example, an employee who had a salary of 300 marks per month before the war, received 100,000 marks in December 1922. But whereas one twenty-fifth of his pre-war salary would have bought him a pair of shoes and one twentieth a set of bed linen, the required proportion of his 1922 salary would be one seventh and one fifth respectively. It is impossible to generalise with any accuracy about the incomes of the self-employed. The stimulus that the Inflation gave to the economy for long periods, the scarcity of goods and the wild scramble for *Sachwerte* enabled many to earn lots of money and to keep their incomes at a high level. Farmers in particular more than managed to preserve their incomes, indeed improved their position. Legitimate business prospered as well. Manufacturers, favoured by the low level of wages, merchants assured of a market for their wares, and all traders in *Sachwerte* flourished in the heated economic climate of the times. But although the profits in paper marks were huge and lavishly spent, keeping those who made them in oysters and champagne, only the clever and smart operators could avoid the dwindling of these paper marks as the mark depreciated more and more rapidly. Often stocks could not be replenished with the proceeds from sales, machinery was not properly maintained, working capital shrank, and, though the businessman had been able to spend and live well with what he took out of his till, he discovered that he had lived on his capital and so become much poorer. Small shopkeepers in particular were affected by this, and, as we have said, many went to the wall. The experience of Hilde Homer's father is a good example of this. He had a shoe shop at 154 Hauptstrasse in Königswinter on the Rhine.

I still remember how one night my father and mother sat up until late as usual, counting the week's takings and stuffing them into potato sacks. I went with father to Cologne early next morning to Herr Guttmann's warehouse where he bought his stock. We were there before it opened, so that we would get in before the banks in their turn opened (the value of money would be down again). I remember the shock of that morning. We were told to dump our precious sacks in a corner with a lot of others. "How much, Herr Cahn?" asked the sales-man. My father told him the amount. "All right, that will buy you five pairs of shoes."

We stopped selling goods for money after that. We bartered them for potatoes, apples, a piece of goat's meat, clothes for the family, coal and wood.

The fortunes of professional people were dependent on those of their clients, and these were often the distressed, old, and middle class. Consequently professional incomes were low. It was not worth litigating about depreciated money, so there was less work for lawyers. Medical care became a luxury for impoverished people; "and I remember", says W.G., "that my dentist had to be content to carry out some complicated dental work for one bottle of mediocre Moselle that still remained in the family cellar."

Dr Barten, an eye surgeon, began to charge his private patients according to the price of food. His widow remembers that he decided that his consultation fee would be the equivalent of a pound of butter. "On one occasion a very elegant patient haggled because the price of butter in the nearby town where she came from was lower!"

Mrs Walker's father, who was a schoolmaster in Frankfurt, tried to add to the family income by giving private lessons.

At first he used to bring the money home, but by the time the family could get to the shops with it, it had lost most of its value. So instead, as soon as he got his fees he went straight across the road to a confectioners and spent them on cream cakes which on his return home he deposited in the letterbox (the

large lockable kind we used to have in Germany).
After dinner he would ask one of us children to go to
the letter box and find his "earnings!"

Significantly enough, painters, sculptors and other
artists did well. Their works were in great demand by the
nouveaux riches in search of inflation-proof investments,
"stable values", to consume the profits they had made
from inflation. These patrons of the arts were not very
great connoisseurs and not too choosy in the selection of
their purchases, and so it happened that second- and
third-rate artists who had been starving in their garrets
joined the ranks of their betters and earned well. Their
prosperity did not survive the stabilisation of the mark. It
had been a typical child of the Inflation, when not only
currency, but also the standards of civilisation in general,
were debased.

Chapter 3

The Winners

One of the most extraordinary aspects of the German Inflation is that, though it was a disaster for the nation, it was a windfall for many of its citizens, a state of affairs that could only carry within itself the seeds of future strife. It was the winners at the inflation game whose activities poisoned not only the relationships between German and German, but also in the long run, between Germany and her neighbours.

To begin in the international field, one way to make money out of the conditions created by the depreciation of the mark was to take advantage of the discrepancy between its internal and external values. Almost for the entire duration of the Inflation, with the exception of the last few months, the internal purchasing power of the mark was higher than its exchange rate in the international currency markets. The mark was undervalued, as the pound was in 1973 (as British ministers never tire of pointing out), only to a much worse degree. Consequently, it was cheap to buy German goods and services with marks acquired in exchange for foreign currency. The first category of Inflation winners is therefore represented by holders of foreign currency.

Foreign currency, of any denomination and from any country, became a national pre-occupation. Mrs Walker, a child in Frankfurt at the time, recalls a child's imaginative impression of the grown-up world.

> We first learned about the inflation through hearing people always talking about *Valuta,* the term for foreign currency. We children had no idea what *Valuta* was, but imagined it to be a lady walking uphill and downhill in a flowing dress, sometimes looking downcast and at others skipping along gaily. This vision was created by hearing the grown-ups saying, *"Die Valuta* is rising", *"Die Valuta* is falling!"

An English journalist, returning to England from a holiday in Austria, broke his journey at Munich for a few days. He related, "One of the principal impressions that remains with me is that of the furtive little men with brief cases waiting outside the railway station and approaching foreign passengers as they emerged: 'You want marks? You want marks?' " When he arrived at his hotel the hall porter told him, "We hall porters are doing well — we get good tips in foreign currency. You will find us in the private boxes at the Opera. We can afford it."

One of the factors that governed the value of the mark abroad was the behaviour of foreign currency exchanges, and in particular of currency dealers in Germany itself.

Foreign exchange speculation, with its resulting damage to the mark, grew out of what was, in fact, a perfectly legitimate activity. Mr C. S., now a member of a merchant bank in London, spent some of his early years as a currency dealer in Berlin during the Inflation. He describes the change that crept into the atmosphere of the most austere and upright profession in Germany:

A banker at that time was usually an elderly man, very conservative in his views, very respectable, talking very slowly and never doing anything on the spur of the moment. The young men came into their own because they had the flair. At that time everything we did on the foreign exchange market was a speculation — whether you bought, whether you sold, whether you waited five minutes — everything was a speculation. You just acted on flair.

But currency dealings had always been a recognised activity and even an important activity, to equalise prices amongst the various currencies on an international basis. It was important — in the days before currency speculation began and when the word inflation hardly existed — that the relationship between the individual currencies should be maintained on a strictly stable basis, and it was the task of the foreign exchange dealer to maintain this relationship as soon as he discovered the slightest discrepancy. What the young men discovered was that when they bought sterling in Austria, for instance — instead of selling it in France and afterwards selling the francs again in Austria to recover their outlay, it paid them much better to keep the sterling and wait until it rose. In this way the activity of the legitimate dealer degenerated into that of a speculator. I learned soon enough what it was all about. Previously we had dealt in very large sums and contented ourselves with a tiny profit which, expressed in terms of percentages, amounted not to a *per cent* but to a fraction of a *per mille.* Now I knew that it was better to buy my sterling and hang on to it for two or three days and make a profit of quite a few per cent.

The real profit came in the end when you kept the final foreign currency after a series of international deals instead of converting it into your own currency. The old-fashioned banker would have strictly forbidden this. I would have got the sack when I worked in Vienna, some years earlier, if I had kept a position open even for a few hours. My books had always to be even. Now, in inflationary Germany, things were changing. A German dealer, by holding on to a foreign currency — no matter what it was, if it had been Siamese it would have been just the same — would make money provided that he held on to it even for one or two days. At the beginning I would be bold enough to keep it for a day or two without telling my boss, and then show him what a wonderful profit I had made. Later on I became bolder and kept it even for a week. That gave you a colossal profit, and that went on and on. And that was why it was a field day for the young people who were a bit more reckless than the old ones whose years of experience made them cautious.

Obviously this kind of speculation damaged the mark, and the astonishing thing is that the Reichsbank allowed this to happen without having the slightest experience of how to stop it. They just sold you the sterling out of the reserves they had.

The thing which, in my opinion, you can always hold against currency speculation, in contrast to Stock–Exchange speculation, is that the speculators in currency can actually make that speculation pay by their own activity.

Not everyone acquired foreign currency by means harmful to the economy. Professor Bonn, the economist, found himself in a privileged position because his English wife had a small sterling income of her own and he himself was very much in demand at that time as a contributor to American newspapers. Mrs Morley got five shillings from an uncle in South Africa and bought a bicycle. The Royal Mail Line in Hamburg paid its apprentices £1 a month in sterling. Countess von Bülow let her house in the Potsdamer Platz in Berlin to the Americans for dollars and retired to the attic to live. Mr Soameson's mother also earned dollars by letting rooms in their flat off the Kurfürstendamm to the Japanese. Further examples of the same type are given in the latter part of the previous chapter. Certainly, those who lived in the capital or in the big ports could take advantage of the presence of foreigners.

There were also a number of operations that took place in a twilight zone of semi-legality. In these, foreign currency did not actually change hands, but the "operator" could nevertheless reap the benefits of a foreign exchange deal. A young man in Silesia in eastern Germany had an advantageous arrangement with a family friend who traded with Czechoslovakia.

As a margarine manufacturer he was licensed to acquire foreign currency for the import of foreign oils and fats. Any surplus marks I had, I used to hand over to him and he would credit me on paper with the equivalent amount of Czech crowns at the going rate of exchange. When I needed to buy some

particular article I would find out the price,
telephone my friend to convert the exact amount of
crowns out of my credit account — not a precious
crown more — into the number of marks I needed. I
would then rush round to his office, grab the marks
and dash back to the shop to make my purchase
before the dollar index changed and the value of my
money fell.

All that did not matter very much so long as such
privileged individuals did not appear in large numbers
and become too conspicuous to the not-so-privileged
German masses. W.G. recalls,

When I was a student in Freiburg only some 30
miles from the Swiss border, there was a regular
influx of visitors from nearby Basle. They were quite
ordinary people, mostly young, who came for a day's
shopping and enjoyment. They filled the best cafés
and restaurants, bought luxury goods, had the
prettiest girls and spent on their pleasures what to
us seemed enormous sums of money though it was
very little in their own hard francs. Most of us had
very little money, lived in rather reduced circumstances and could never afford to see the inside of all
those glamorous places into which the foreigners
crowded. Of course we were envious, at the same
time developing as a sort of defence mechanism a
pride in being poor. And this contempt for the rich
visitors combined with suppressed envy to produce
in most of us a great deal of xenophobia and
nationalist feeling, a fertile breeding ground for the
incipient Nazi movement.

In an odd way the Nazis themselves profited from the

depreciation of the currency, which they so vociferously denounced as the work of Jewish speculators and the new democratic State. The young party was short of cash and relied very much on voluntary contributions from sympathisers, of whom plenty were to be found abroad, in countries with strong currencies. There were, for instance, the Sudeten Germans in Czechoslovakia, and other sympathisers in Switzerland, the United States and elsewhere who contributed freely to the party funds. And although the number of francs and dollars and crowns they sent may have been small, they reprensented huge sums of marks which went to swell the Nazi fighting funds; after all, as Konrad Heiden, who recalls this fact, remarks, "For 100 dollars one could buy a minor revolution."

The impact of this, though important in other respects, was in strictly economic terms minor. But possession of foreign currency could also buy real economic power on the cheap. What happened in Germany has been called a gigantic clearance sale, and, though this might have been an exaggeration, containing an element of nationalist propaganda, there is no doubt that foreigners with their own currency did in fact acquire a considerable amount of wealth in Germany, especially property and shares in limited companies. It has been estimated that by 1923 foreigners had acquired 10 per cent of the total share capital of German businesses. The value of house property bought by foreigners is said to have amounted to several milliard gold marks; 25,000 houses in Berlin alone passed into foreign ownership. Again, these estimates are to be taken with a pinch of salt, but it was only too obvious to anybody who lived in Germany at the time that the sales of property to foreigners were indeed on a staggering scale.

The Great Inflation

It is a fact that some foreign students at German universities bought out of their monthly allowances entire streets of houses. In this, they were favoured not only by the exchange, but also by the depressed prices that property, for reasons we have explained, commanded at that time.

> Several years after the Inflation, when I was a lawyer in Berlin (relates W.G.), one of my clients was a Spanish doctor, then resident in Madrid or Barcelona, who owned a number of valuable tenement houses in Berlin which he had acquired when he was a medical student at Berlin University. He had paid a pittance for them, and was now a rich landlord.

For the foreign buyer such an acquisition was of course a speculation, but that was the very essence of any transaction aiming at Inflation profits: the operator had to either anticipate — "speculate on" — a continuing decline of the currency or estimate that the prices of *Sachwerte,* depressed by circumstances peculiar to the inflation period, would in due course rise again. It is interesting to note that agricultural land, the price of which more or less kept pace with the Inflation, was rarely involved in these purchases; foreign buyers concentrated instead on urban property. Here their stakes were very small, and they could afford to have the nerve and the patience to wait for better days.

When, in 1922, these property sales became more frequent and caused a scandal, legislative measures were taken to restrict the trade; but, by the interposition of men of straw, the formation of limited companies and similar devices, determined foreign purchasers largely succeeded in circumventing the restrictions.

Foreigners could take advantage of having a stronger currency, even in quite ordinary business. For instance, the British publishers George Allen and Unwin had books printed in Germany and, by paying for the work in cheaply acquired marks, got them for a fraction of what the job would have cost if the work had been done in England.

German citizens involved in big business and having foreign currency at their disposal were able to cash in on this advantage in a massive way. The export trade, favoured by the peculiar circumstances of the Inflation, flourished, and large amounts of foreign currency flowed into the hands of firms engaged in this trade. The money was supposed to be used for the urgent requirements of the national economy, but, legitimately or not, parts of it were hoarded by the recipients for later use.

Some of Germany's big industrialists had owned huge industrial properties, such as iron and steel works, coal mines, and the like, in Lorraine, the Saarland and Luxembourg. After the war these properties passed into French hands, the former owners receiving compensation partly from the Reich, which represented a most useful addition to their financial strength, but partly also in French currency, which vastly increased their foreign currency resources. All things considered, these men never neglected any opportunity for acquiring foreign currency, regardless of the consequences such actions might have for the national interest. When, for instance, during the occupation of the Ruhr, the Reichsbank desperately tried to support the collapsing mark by selling its carefully hoarded reserves, the firm of Hugo Stinnes did not hesitate to buy up as much of them as it could to bolster up the Stinnes currency hoard. How this was done remains somewhat obscure, in spite of a Parliamentary inquiry that took place in summer 1923 and sought to throw some light on the affair. Certainly, Stinnes was able to import English coal, which was urgently needed as Ruhr coal was no longer available, and to make huge profits.

Foreign earnings converted at an opportune moment and quickly spent on the purchase of low-priced German goods for export yielded handsome profits, indeed a double profit: one on the mark-up charged to the foreign buyer in hard currency, and another resulting from paying the supplier in cheaply acquired marks. It is not difficult to see what was meant by the "dance of the parities"!

But the proceeds from the export trade not only served to keep that trade going and growing. Some of them were used to buy up more businesses — more *Sachwerte* — inside Germany, thus enlarging the economic power basis of the entrepreneur. But the really big operators of foreign currency deals did not confine their interests to their own country. With the foreign currency they had at their disposal, they were able to do what was well-nigh impossible for the ordinary German: spend money abroad, invest and accumulate capital outside their own country. This they did with a vengeance; and the millions they accumulated were in good money. Here, of course, the reward was not produced by skilfully playing on the "dance of the parities", but by taking advantage of the opportunities for tucking away capital far from the uncertainties of a Germany threatened by chaos, and by widening the entrepreneur's power basis beyond the confines of Germany and building business empires of international importance — something like the "multi-nationals" of the present day.

Perhaps the *reductio ad absurdum* of the whole mystique of foreign currency during the Inflation can be expressed by some recollections of Leopold Ullstein, whose family owned one of the largest publishing houses in Europe:

> My brother had been to Spain in connection with some family business there. On his return he happened to find a small piece of change in his pocket which he had overlooked — a silver coin. I still remember him showing it to us — this tremendous thing, a silver coin, which had assumed a sort of magic spell. He was juggling with it in his fingers as he showed it around, when suddenly there was a shout! There was a small crack between the door and the wall in the living-room and this peseta or whatever it was had rolled into it. There then began a great family argument about whether the door frame should be removed or the wall pulled down to get at it!

But the king of all currencies was the dollar. Leopold Ullstein relates,

> Our cook had been with us for ten years and my mother was anxious to mark the occasion by making her a suitable present. My brother-in-law had got hold of a dollar — one single dollar — and it was seriously considered that this would be the best present that one could make to this faithful servant. But then objections were raised. She was indeed a magnificent cook, but she was too simple and unsophisticated to handle such a fortune. The only way would be to set up a trust fund at the bank to administer the dollar for her!

The Great Inflation

Mrs Ehrhardt, whose widowed mother somehow brought up four children in Berlin during the Inflation years, sums up once and for all this terrible "dollar-mania" which gripped everyone, high or low, rich or poor:

> Long afterwards I referred to the Inflation in my mother's hearing as the time when one actually contemplated murder just to get hold of a dollar. She looked very much struck by my words and said I had described the spirit of the time exactly — and she was the best Christian woman I have ever met.

The other road to riches in a country affected by inflation is simply to owe money. To be a debtor under the rule that "the mark of yesterday equals the mark of today" ("mark equals mark") meant being able to discharge a debt at the exact figure shown in the contract by paying it off with an equivalent amount of depreciated paper marks. There were two ways in which this situation could be exploited: first, by getting rid of old debts, some contracted before the war, the diminished or vanished value of which was obvious even to a simpleton; secondly, by contracting new debts, taking advantage of the ease with which credit — and cheap credit at that — was obtainable. The debt would then be repaid after the hoped-for depreciation of the mark had materialised.

But whether the stakes were small or big, to succeed in the game it was necessary to understand the nature of the Inflation and to foresee, or guess correctly, the future course it would take. In some cases and in minor ways that was easy: it needed no great business or financial acumen, and certainly no daring, for the Swiss or Dutch visitor to Germany to see that he could obtain tremendous bargains even though the price tags showed ever-growing numbers of noughts. In a similar case in 1973, the housewives of Boulogne flocked to Folkestone on a cross-channel trip to buy cheaply in British supermarkets and chain stores, thereby taking advantage of inflation-ridden Britain and her depreciated currency.

But when it came to business — big business often on a gigantic scale — the essentials for success were fore-sight, strong nerves, a clear reading both of the signs pointing to *Sachwerte* and of the direction the Inflation was taking, and, in addition, a certain lack of scruples. The "dance of the parities", it might be said, took place on a slippery parquet floor, and only the clever and the ruthless, sober in spite of the heady wine of enormous figures, were able to keep their balance and to excel in the dancing competition.

Even people who had lifelong business experience and were anything but "little men" did not understand the nature of the Inflation and fell victim to the confusion of the times and the "revaluation of all values". Their failures and losses were transformed directly into the successes and gains of the stronger ones.

The story is in essence the same as that of the owners of rented property. Like them, these less-adaptable businessmen were dazzled by the large amounts of marks offered to them for their enterprises, unaware of the low "real value" of the price. They were unwilling or unable to cope with the difficulties of the turbulent times and happy in the illusion that they had received fabulous fortunes for what they considered an embarrassment and a burden.

Lisa Frank's father is an example of this sort of tragedy. He was a lithographer and was at an age where it was beyond his mental agility to grasp the implications of inflation. As he had to replace his stocks of paper at higher and higher prices, he found himself constantly having to justify the increased charges to his customers. For a man of 70 it was all too much. He decided to escape his troubles by selling up his business. His daughter begged him not to.

> I was only too aware of what was going on all around us, but my father said, "You are too young, you don't understand". Then one day I came home from the bank to find that he had sold everything — shop and factory — for 6 million marks. He would never have to work again, he said. Alas, he very soon discovered his terrible mistake and never recovered from it. A series of strokes brought him to his grave within two years.

In this way the "big boys" managed to buy up whole assortments of enterprises and valuable *Sachwerte*.

The little boys, too, were quick to see how advantage could be taken of adult bewilderment. H. G. Soameson was a schoolboy in Berlin. All his classmates had found some sort of racket for making money: his own was bookselling.

> It was idiotic those days. People just couldn't keep track of the prices. My dodge was to buy all the literature books in the school bookshop, where prices were low anyway, and sell them at a nice profit to an antiquarian bookseller five minutes away.
>
> On another occasion I remember buying at Wertheims [the equivalent of Selfridges] the collected works of an author called (if I remember

correctly) Conradi, in five volumes. I don't know who he was — I never read him — but the books were beautifully bound in blue linen. I took them, brand-new from the store and sold them to a second-hand bookseller in the street — at a profit!

Günther Porton-Seigne, the young apprentice in a transport firm, also found a way to beat the system:

I came to an agreement with the manager whereby I was paid on Monday instead of on Friday. At that time I was attending night-school and one of my classmates worked for Sarotti, the big chocolate firm. I used to buy 30 or 40 bars of chocolate from him, cash down, and hold them until the following Saturday. Then I sold them to our local grocer for the going rate, thereby making three or four times my wages within the week. With these "earnings" I bought butter, fats, flour and noodles and gave them to my mother as my contribution to the household. This contribution was worth many times more than that of my hard-working father.

I eventually confessed to the manager how I was manipulating my Monday salary. He told me later that he had taken the tip from me and had done the same thing with his brother-in-law, who worked for a cigarette firm.

Another ingredient of success in the inflation stakes was credit: to be — at least in the economic sense — a person of good character and sound financial standing, and thus, command the trust of those able to lend. To enjoy credit is most important and profitable in times of currency depreciation, and this truism holds good for the inflation of our own time. In the autumn of 1973 it was a much discussed fact that "blue chip" companies in Britain utilised their credit to borrow large amounts of money, not for their genuine financial requirements but in order to lend it at higher rates of interest to other firms not so well placed to borrow direct from the big banks. As the very high interest rates then prevailing were, in fact, at least partial compensation for the actual or anticipated depreciation of the pound, the margin that the primary borrowers earned was sheer profit based on their credit-worthiness and good standing with the big banks.

Inflationary gains made out of the decline of the mark were, if technically different, basically of the same type. "Industry rapidly recognised," reported the German Bankers' Association in 1923, "that it was economically more advantageous to incur the highest possible debts at the bank rather than to keep large deposits." It was indeed, to put it more bluntly, the banks' generosity in supplying credit that opened golden opportunities for speculating on the further fall of the mark and thereby amassing fortunes.

Many of these speculators did not hesitate to *corriger la fortune;* that is, improve their chance of making money out of the decline of the mark by selling borrowed marks on the international exchange markets, thus precipitating the downward trend and putting themselves in a position to repay their debts at an even lower and more profitable rate.

The credit-worthiness of these people was mainly due to the fact that they were already rich and financially important men when, after the war, the inflation inherited from it began slowly to gain momentum. They were the armament manufacturers, the merchants of

104

death, the providers of the scarce raw materials needed to keep the war machine going. Usually they had been wealthy even before the war started, but they multiplied their fortunes in what was for them the enormous sellers' market of the war economy, often extending their business activities into the (for them) very favourable conditions in the parts of France, Belgium and Russia occupied and administered by Germany. They were among the privileged few able to carry on an import and export business, though it was severely curtailed by the wartime blockade and limited to the few still accessible neutral countries. This trade was not only a source of profit, but it also opened the eyes of these businessmen at an early stage to the erosion of the German currency and the opportunities that it would offer.

During the great German Inflation, the system of "through credit to riches" was all-pervading and worked on all levels, from tiny everyday transactions to the financier's gigantic coup. The ability to obtain credit was even better than the licence to print money; for those that had it could even save the bother and expense of the actual printing and could receive the money, ready-made, from the bank.

W.G. remembers an illuminating example of a small-scale operation of this kind:

> In the summer of 1923, when the Inflation had already reached its galloping stage, my brother got married and the wedding was celebrated in Munich, at the best hotel in the city, the *Vier Jahreszeiten*. It was a sumptuous feast, with the best food, finest wines, champagne, the lot. This was possible because Uncle Max, a brother of the bride's father, owned a wine and spirit business which had

prospered wonderfully during the Inflation and for this he was allocated a quota of foreign currency. Uncle Max paid the bill — a fair number of millions — by a cheque drawn on his Berlin bank account. It took some time before the cheque was presented and when it was finally cleared the actual price Uncle Max had to pay for his avuncular generosity amounted to something like a couple of dollars.

The mirror image, so to speak, of this story, can be found in one of Alexander Woollcott's famous broadcasts, "The Mysteries of Rudolfo", which concerned Herr Rudolf Kommer, a writer and journalist living in America: Kommer was very successful as a translator of English plays into German, and his greatest success in the German-speaking world, the comedy *Potash and Perlmutter*, was a stage hit on both sides of the Atlantic. "It did heap up", Mr Woollcott reports, "a very mountain of marks, awaiting his pleasure, but before he got around to collecting them the value of the mark had fallen to almost nothing at all, so that his greatest triumph yielded him one dollar and ninety-eight cents."

Typical is the story told by a German landowner who, having come into possession of a large estate during the Inflation, had to restock it. He bought, on credit, a whole herd of valuable cattle. After a certain time he sold one cow from the herd. Because of depreciation of the mark, the price he got for it was sufficient to pay off the cost of the whole herd.

A more questionable form of enrichment was made possible by the working of the German tax system. Employees paid income tax on their earnings through a kind of pay-as-you-earn system; that is to say, the employer withheld a percentage of the wages to be passed on to the tax authorities in due course. "In due course" is the operative phrase, because, before he was called upon to pay it, the employer enjoyed the tax money as a free loan with which he could buy goods and raw materials, in short *Sachwerte,* and then hand over to the tax collector valueless pieces of paper. (At times it needed only a few days to reduce the money to that state, but in actual fact the intervening period — which could be regarded as the duration of the loan — was usually much longer.) The sad aspect of that practice is not so much that the State lost its revenue (although that was serious enough), but that the employer enriched himself to the detriment of the employee, who, at the time the tax was deducted, could have bought with it enough food to improve his own low standard of living.

The vast sums of money invested by the public in war loans, State and municipal bonds, mortgages and similar fixed money securities were wiped out by the collapse of the mark. Conversely the Reich, provinces, municipalities and all those institutions that had borrowed these moneys got rid of their indebtedness at the expense of their creditors, whose plight will be described in a later chapter. To that extent they were able to chalk up a profit on their accounts and rank among the Inflation winners.

The story of their gains, however enormous the sums involved, is a somewhat monotonous one. Much more amusing and colourful is that of the accumulation of gigantic fortunes which private entrepreneurs achieved by skilfully exploiting the chances offered by the Inflation.

It would be unfair to deny to at least some of them sound ideas about concentration and rationalisation of trade and industry, which motivated their operations.

Their particular genius was that they recognised at an early stage of the Inflation the shift in values, a potential gold-mine for those able to exploit it in their business transactions. Money was becoming much less important than *Sachwerte* — real values. These men were the heralds of the flight from money into *Sachwerte,* and what made their moves so profitable was that they were largely carried out on credit. That was the main secret of their success. One of them, Otto Wolff, is quoted as having said, "I am not yet quite as big as Herr Stinnes — but I am already in debt to the tune of several milliards!"

So they bought up steelworks, shipyards, shipping lines, coal-mines, banks — in short every imaginable kind of enterprise — sometimes persuading a less clever owner to sell direct, sometimes gaining control through ingenious Stock–Exchange operations; operations that would not have been possible without the Inflation and would have landed the speculators in the bankruptcy court. The Inflation helped them because "real" share prices were low and, moreover, the speculators were able to work profitable miracles by the magic of credit. Sometimes, though not always, they bought quite indiscriminately in order to build up their empires. These became, in truth, just "department stores of *Sachwerte",* in the same way that minor inflation profiteers invested in anything from waste paper to jewellery and second-class paintings.

To obtain the necessary credit was child's play for these men, who had achieved in various ways the status of "men of property" and the credit-worthiness that went with it. The banks were only too eager to oblige. As we have seen, the Reichsbank lent money at the rate of 5 per cent until July 1922, raising the rate gradually to as little as 30 per cent in August 1923, and in September 1923 to

90 per cent — chicken-feed for the borrower who could repay the loan with depreciated money. The niceties of the banking business — that there must be some collateral for credits — were still observed, but that was no problem. For instance, it is recounted that Friedrich Flick, one of the most powerful figures in the world of iron and steel, having acquired the share capital of one company, offered these shares as collateral, to borrow the cash with which to acquire a second and third company and so on.

An insider's view of how such an Inflation empire was built is revealing. Herbert Hochfeld, who was earning his "rye" wages on a farm, saw that same farm grow into what we would today call a conglomerate. Although the point of departure was not industrial but agricultural, and development was on a comparatively small scale, it is a characteristic example of the compulsive, almost automatic force of the Inflation leading to the accumulation of wealth. For Herbert Hochfeld it was also a stark contrast with his own circumstances.

> My father was a doctor, and the time-lag between bills presented and fees paid meant that his income lagged behind the Inflation. He died, leaving no money, and I had to find a job quickly. I got work on a nearby farm. My employer had acquired a large estate with cattle, crops and forests for hunting. Consequently he had a continuing supply of *Sachwerte* in the form of wheat, rye and meat. He was shrewd in business and began to amass a great deal of money, which he used for expanding his business. He expanded vertically, as it were. First of all he bought a fleet of lorries so that he could transport as much grain as possible to the port. This

109

brought him more money so he went on to buy a fleet of ships for exporting his grain from Hamburg to Norway. There was no point in putting any of his profits into a bank, or into any other form of saving, so all he could do was expand, expand, expand, and the whole thing became an empire.

The main explanation of the fact that the agriculturists were amongst the "winners" is simple: the cancellation of their indebtedness by depreciation. German agricultural property before the war was mortgaged to the tune of a total of about 15 milliard gold marks, a burden of which they rid themselves. But in the meantime the payment of interest, which constituted a constant drain on their incomes, dwindled rapidly and became insignificant, while their incomes themselves remained more or less stable, the real prices for agricultural produce, with certain interruptions, remaining almost at world price levels. To illustrate this: the total sum of mortgage interests due amounted to some 600 million marks; in 1913 that was the equivalent of 4 million tons of rye; already in 1921 it could be paid with the proceeds of the sale of 200,000 tons.

Having a stable income, owners of agricultural land were, unlike the owners of urban property, neither tempted nor forced to sell. Indeed, the very high prices of such properties — high reckoned in gold marks — were a deterrent to speculators and the number of such properties that changed hands during the Inflation was relatively small.

Farmers had certain technical difficulties in converting the paper money they received for their produce into real values. To be sure, they had learned rather early the value of *Sachwerte,* and the money that came in — often originating in black-market transactions — was used to purchase not only new machinery and buildings, but also assortments of pianos (never played), canteens of cutlery (never used at table), carpets, furniture, gramophones, diamonds, and so on and so on. But as the pace of the Inflation quickened, problems of timing made it more difficult for farmers to take full advantage of the opportunities the Inflation offered. By the nature of their business, money came in at fixed periods determined by the seasons and the harvests, and the distance of farms from financial and commercial centres made more difficult the rapid conversion of these monies into stable values.

There were many well-known characters among the Inflation profiteers and the majority have sunk into oblivion, if only because they were unable to survive the end of those extraordinary circumstances that had swept them to wealth and fame — or notoriety. Some of the names, however, still linger on in the memories of Germans who lived through the period, or in the pages of contemporary writings: Otto Wolff, Friedrich Flick, Friedrich Minoux, Hugo I. Herzfeld, Siegmund Bosel, Camillo Castiglioni, Alfred Hugenberg. But the giant among the men who built economic empires on the slippery foundation of the collapsing mark, the very king of the Inflation, was the legendary figure of Hugo Stinnes. When he died in 1924, within a few months of the stabilisation of the mark, and still in his early fifties, it was the end of an era of which he was the symbol.

He was a man of extremely simple tastes, a family man who did not smoke and hardly ever took any alcohol, though he consumed vast quantities of coffee and tea to keep him awake during his excessive working hours. He was a notoriously bad dresser. Viscount D'Abernon, the

111

British Ambassador, who admitted not liking him, talked of his "bedraggled, untidy look as of a rough-haired terrier just come out of one scrap and in search of another". With his unfashionable "Assyrian" beard he cut an unworldly figure among his high-living contemporaries and in the luxury hotels, notably the elegant "Esplanade" in Berlin, where he stayed. He stayed in such hotels mainly for the simple reason that he owned them, and here, somewhat ostentatiously, he displayed his modesty by registering as Hugo Stinnes, merchant from Mülheim-an-der-Ruhr.

Stinnes had made himself the richest man in Germany, with a personal fortune estimated at several hundred million gold marks and control over wealth to the tune of many milliard gold marks: more, it was said, than the fabulous fortunes of the Carnegies, Rockefellers and Vanderbilts amounted to.

The total number of enterprises over which Stinnes ruled is somewhat obscure, doubtless kept so for reasons of taxation. But it is safe to say that it was well in excess of 4,000; 4,554 according to Stinnes's biographer, Gert von Klass.

It was a veritable "department store of enterprises", an apparently higgledy-piggledy list of accumulated assets which makes the mind boggle. There were coal-mines and sanatoria, steelworks and cigarette factories, oil-wells and refineries, cinemas, newspapers, shipping lines, paper mills, tanneries, blast furnaces, margarine factories, banks, hotels, electricity generating plants, forests, printing plants and building firms. There were aluminium works in Italy, sawmills in Romania, metallurgical works in Russia, ironworks in Austria, sugar factories in Czechoslovakia, petrol concerns in Argentina. Altogether, Stinnes's business interests outside Germany numbered 572, and extended, apart from the already mentioned countries, to Hungary, Poland, Scandinavia, Britain, Holland, Belgium and Luxembourg, France, Spain, Portugal, Switzerland, North and South America, Japan, China and Persia. All that, it may be noted in passing, had had to be acquired with the most precious, the most sought-after, that almost magic thing that existed in the Germany of the Inflation: foreign currency.

Crazy as this accumulation may appear, there was a lot of method in such madness.

Stinnes was born in 1870 as the scion of a wealthy family in the coal and transport business. He was a rich man in his own right when the war started. He grew richer during the war as supplier and importer of materials needed for the war effort and also as an exploiter of industries in the German-occupied territories.

His power basis, besides his coal and transport interests, was the Siemens-Rheinelbe-Schuckert Union, which was a vast combine of mining, iron and steel and electrical industries. It was a vertical concentration of enterprises, the idea being that the whole process of production from raw material to finished article should be controlled by one organisation, without being dependent on the purchase of any intermediate products from outsiders.

Stinnes had the genius to visualise the economic advantages of such rationalisation and with this he combined the foresight and understanding that in a time of depreciating money the acquisition of *Sachwerte* was the sole guarantee of staying in business and prospering. So he set out to acquire anything that was for sale and seemed to fit into his schemes, adding to the satellites

113

surrounding his sun, the original source of economic energy. So the coal trade led to coal-mining, coal-mines needing pit props to the acquisition of forests, forests to cellulose factories, manufacture of paper, printing plants, newspapers and publishing. His interests in transport and inland shipping on the one hand, and in iron and steel on the other, converged in the incorporation of shipyards into his empire and, as a second stage, trans-oceanic shipping lines, passenger transport, and investment in the hotel and restaurant business. And so it went on. There was indeed method in this madness, but an element of straightforward madness seemingly remained and engendered that furious energy, which ultimately the whole nation shared with him, for buying up and accumulating *Sachwerte*. The result was the failure to create that solidly based, organic whole at which he had aimed; a failure that proved fatal when the special conditions of the Inflation ceased and the organising genius who might have found ways of weathering the storm was dead.

In Hugo Stinnes were combined all the prerequisites for an Inflation profiteer. He had the wealth, founded before the war and much enlarged during it, as well as the ability to read the signs of the times and so see how to swim safely and successfully through the turbulent waters of the Inflation. He recognised before his contemporaries the phenomenon born of the Inflation: that industrial shares, commercial enterprises, all kinds of assets were cheap, and that their owners, confused and frightened by the prevailing conditions, could be persuaded to part with them at bargain prices. He pounced on these chances like the accomplished asset-stripper of our days, reforming, transforming and combining these acquisitions with great profit. More important, he commanded almost unlimited credit, with which he could finance such operations — it would happen that he bought a particular object not because he wanted it, but simply because he had some spare credit at his disposal — and one need not reiterate how fantastically rewarding such transactions were.

In addition he had the most precious fuel for the money-making machinery: *Devisen, Valuta* — in other words, foreign currency. This came from the sale of foreign assets, from the export trade, from shipping, from the revenues of foreign investments — and came in vast quantities. In a dollar-starved Germany this raised Stinnes to commanding heights, a position comparable to that of an Arab oil sheikh in an energy crisis. Profits were there for the taking.

One can only guess how profitable it was to shift moneys between the various outposts of his far-flung empire (just as the so-called multinationals can do today), to buy back marks at the right moment and invest them in good time. More obvious, more normal as it were, were the possibilities for enlarging trade with foreign countries, a privilege not enjoyed by everybody. It enabled Stinnes, for instance, to carry out a transaction already mentioned — the import of British coal during the Ruhr crisis. It was his biggest, but certainly not his only, deal of this kind; and by investing abroad he was able to broaden his empire — and his source of dollars.

Stinnes had, in a paternalistic way, a social conscience. After the November revolution he was instrumental in setting up a joint organisation of employers and workers to improve relations between the two sides of industry: he even named one of his ships after a prominent German trade-union leader — Carl Legien. He saw the need for higher wages. But if he accepted the increase in wages and other production costs as an inevitable consequence of the Inflation, he managed to turn this into an additional profit. Capable of reckoning in real money, he increased his prices not only by the amount of the original cost, but also by rounding them up and charging high premiums for anticipated depreciation costs, thereby considerably increasing his real income whilst real wages did not rise in harmony.

Stinnes considered inflation necessary in the conditions in which Germany found itself after the war. On 22nd June 1922, in a conversation he had with the American Ambassador in Berlin and some others about the reasons why Germany carried on the inflation policy, he spelled out his ideas: "I pointed out", he wrote in a memorandum afterwards, "that after a lost war it was absolutely necessary to bring back four million men . . . into the regular routine of useful activity . . . I also informed the gentlemen that the *weapon of inflation* would have to be used in future . . . because only that made it possible to give the population orderly and regular activity which was necessary to preserve the life of the nation." It was, of course, a case of what was good for Germany was good for Stinnes and his ilk.

Stinnes was not alone in making pronouncements of this kind. The head of the big Klöckner mining and iron and steel combine called the consequences of a rising mark "a disaster of incredible magnitude". A colleague of his said, "Any further improvement in the mark would paralyse exports and provoke vast unemployment."

Whether the German Republic, the Weimar democracy, and its prestige were harmed by his actions did not concern him very much. He had no scruples about exploiting for his own advantage the Ruhr crisis and the Reichsbank's sales of foreign currency in support of the sinking mark. He bought more foreign currency, depressing the mark even further, and enlarging his holdings in this precious commodity. His acquisition of investments abroad at a time when Germany was insisting on her inability to pay reparations angered the Allies, made them doubt Germany's sincerity and hardened their attitudes towards her; and this, in turn, added momentum to Germany's distress.

When, in July 1920, Stinnes participated in the International Conference at Spa as a representative of German industry, the well-known facts of his business activities, combined with the arrogance of his behaviour at the conference, put the Allies' backs up even more.

It cannot be said that he actually conspired to undermine the young democratic State, using the "weapon of inflation" for the purpose. In politics he was a member of the Reichstag, belonging to the moderately right-wing German People's Party. He had been a nationalist and a supporter of German expansionism during the war, and a nationalist he remained; opposed, unless it interfered with his business, to the policies of compliance with the Allies' demands and reconciliation between Germany and her former enemies. He fought the fiscal measures and more stringent taxation proposed by the parties of the Left. A powerful instrument for the propagation of his economic and political aims was the collection of newspapers and other information media that he controlled, having acquired these almost incidentally to the building of his economic empire. He owned some daily papers — the *Deutsche Allgemeine Zeitung* and *Frankfurter Nachrichten*; also a satirical paper, magazines, trade papers, news agencies, publicity agencies and printing plants. These publications were certainly not supporters of any left-wing tendencies or

117

liberal and progressive ideologies. Moreover, these Stinnes interests were closely connected with Alfred Hugenberg — a former director of Krupps. He was a prominent exponent of right-wing radicalism and uncompromising hostility towards the democratic State, and had, with the help of inflationary profits, become the master of a powerful press group which reflected and propagated his anti-Weimar policies. Numerous provincial papers, once liberal or non-party, had become, under his aegis, nationalist. He also owned the famous Ufa, the leading enterprise in the German film industry.

It was one of the paradoxes of the Inflation that both the losers and the winners were united in their hostility towards the new Republic, Weimar, and that there was a sort of cross-fertilisation between the two poles.

The impoverished middle classes forgot all their natural resentment of the biggest of the profiteers to have accumulated fortunes at their expense, and they supported their political aims. The profiteers made ample use of their inflation-born fortunes to campaign against the Republic and to propagate their aims and find electoral support among the new poor. Whether or not they actually conspired to stir up the fires of inflation so that they could burn down the edifice of the Republic, they certainly reckoned that this would, in fact, be the result of the Inflation.

Take the case of Friedrich Minoux, who had been Stinnes's chief lieutenant, had parted company from him in 1923, and was then in his own right an Inflation tycoon of great wealth. In the autumn of 1923, when the mark was in its death throes and chaos and distress reigned in Germany, Minoux was actively participating in preparations for a *coup d'état* aimed at replacing the democratic constitution by a "Directory" (on the model of the

French Revolution), in which Minoux himself would hold a leading position. These were the days preceding Hitler's famous "Bierkeller Putsch". The putsch ultimately failed because a member of a group in Munich that pursued aims similar to those of Minoux's group which he had been despatched to Berlin to consult, was cynically advised by Minoux to wait a little, until the hunger, cold and misery produced by the Inflation then pervading Germany had reached the point of exasperating the masses and making them ripe for revolution!

The struggle against the Republic was conducted by yet another group of "winners" — the so-called "Green Front", which consisted of owners of agricultural land, especially the large proprietors. Their organisation, the Landbund, acted as the instrument for exerting political pressure; it gave them, as the liberal *Berliner Tageblatt* commented on 15th August 1924, "donations in stable values. By such means enormous sums have been collected and have been well used. In all Pomerania there does not exist a newspaper of any importance which does not belong to the Landbund."

Stinnes had expressed the wish that his funeral should be celebrated with all the pomp and circumstance worthy of a king. So, when he died in April 1924, there were flowers worth many thousands of gold marks, and his chief lieutenants, the captains of his ships, the miners of his coal-mines, were in attendance, all solemnly dressed up for the occasion. Yet by the time of his death the stabilisation of the mark had already struck a terrible blow at the edifice he had erected, and the ceremonies on the occasion might have been planned for the funeral pyre of Mammon himself. It is one of the ironies of history that, within the space of a few months, Hugo Stinnes, the greatest beneficiary of the Inflation, was

The Great Inflation

followed to the grave by Rudolf Havenstein, the President of the Reichsbank who had been mainly responsible for the monetary policies of the period, and Karl Helfferich, the wartime Secretary of the Treasury who had initiated the methods of financing the war by borrowing, the root cause of the Inflation.

Chapter 4
The Losers

"The thing was, to try not to become bitter, when you saw other people drinking champagne and making the best of it when you hadn't enough to eat." Mrs Barten's husband was an eye surgeon, and her family is an example of how winners and losers could coexist in the same family.

My husband set up in practice in a small town in East Prussia soon after the war, just as the Inflation was in its early stages, and we married in 1919. My father had given me a good dowry, which included a 30,000 mark mortgage. However, 80 per cent of my husband's patients were "insurance" patients, whose fees were paid by the government. But they were only paid every quarter, and as the Inflation progressed we were virtually without an income. My brother-in-law had a distillery which made liqueurs and, like all businessmen, was well off. My sister-in-law and I had our first babies within a few days of each other and I remember how I was lying in a

121

borrowed iron bedstead with my baby in a borrowed cradle, while she had everything for herself and her baby in pure silk. And yet we both came from the same sort of family background.

I remember how my husband set out to take the tram to visit a patient and had to come back home again because he just hadn't enough to pay for the tram ticket. And I remember how, for me, the last straw was when I went to the shoemakers to collect a pair of shoes I'd had heeled and I hadn't enough money. I ran home and threw myself on my husband's neck, sobbing, because we couldn't even pay for a simple thing like that. In 1923, when things were at their worst, I had a letter from the woman who was paying off the mortgage which was part of my dowry. She paid it off in full, and the money I got just paid for a fortnight's holiday in a cheap boarding house for myself and my baby son.

That I had to put my first child in a borrowed pram, that I couldn't pay for a pair of shoes to be heeled, that my husband had to get down from the tram — these things I can never forget.

It is often said that the worst consequence of the great German Inflation was the destruction of the German middle class. This is much too sweeping a statement, a generalisation that does not bear scrutiny. If one defines — very vaguely — as members of the German middle classes those who had a comfortable income of, say, between 4,000 and 20,000 gold marks per annum, backed by some capital, anything up to a half a million perhaps, and were usually but not necessarily of a certain educational standard, it is not true that all these people were ruined as a result of the Inflation. The agricultural middle classes were certainly not harmed by the Inflation. The same is true of the commercial middle classes, for while many individuals belonging to that category can be counted among the victims, they were replaced by newcomers who, being better equipped to cope with the difficulties of the period, had been able to improve their standing.

What is true is that a sector of the middle class, including many whose financial standing had been even more favourable than indicated above, was utterly ruined by the depreciation of the mark, by "the vastest expropriation", as it has been called, "that has ever been effected in peacetime".

These people included pensioners and the owners of capital who received incomes expressed in fixed money values. Such sources of income included life insurance policies, State securities, municipal and other bonds, war loan and mortgages, to name only the most important. In other words, they had claims against debtors — the State, municipalities, owners of mortgaged property and so on — for a determined sum of marks. As the respective debtors, on the principle of "mark equals mark", were entitled to discharge debts by paying one mark, regardless of its real value, for every mark owed, the expropriation was just a consequence of the dwindling and ultimately vanishing value of the paper mark.

These, then, were the principal and direct losers of the Inflation. Their vicissitudes, together with those of a group that shared their fate though for different reasons — the owners of property for letting — form the subject of this chapter. The story of these victims of the Inflation is important, not so much for the magnitude of the number involved, but for the social and political attitudes consequent upon their fate.

The Great Inflation

The German middle class investor, the *rentier* or any other small capitalist, was rather reluctant to buy industrial shares and preferred investments of the fixed-value type. The total sum so invested before the war is estimated to have exceeded 100 milliard gold marks, and although, of course, only a part of that belonged to individual middle-class holders, the total sum eroded by the Inflation was enormous. After the stabilisation of the mark, the so-called revaluation laws provided some meagre compensation for those who had suffered. But, even so, the measure of their losses was colossal, as emerges from an estimate given by Professor Bonn: the total income of the German *rentier* class before the war had amounted to some 8 milliard gold marks; in 1925 it was 300 million, i.e. some 3 or 4 per cent of the pre-war sum.

Unless he could look forward to a State or a private pension, the ordinary, prudent family man would, as a matter of course, save all his working life in order to provide for his old age and his family. Life insurance was very popular and so were savings banks and similar institutions; and, if he had a business, he would naturally seek to increase its value with a view to later sale and retirement. He would aim at accumulating a capital of, say, 100,000 to 200,000 marks, which would secure for him a modestly comfortable retirement. Accumulated cash would then be invested in house property and interest-bearing bonds of all kinds. During the war, under the impact of patriotism and public pressure, and also because it gave a fair return, much money was put into war loan. In addition, there was a great deal of investment in mortgages, either through the acquisition of mortgage bonds issued by the mortgage banks (the equivalent of building societies) or, very frequently, by

124

direct loans, secured by mortgage, to individual property owners. Here the pattern was that the first mortgage would be held by the mortgage bank, and the second, usually favoured by a higher rate of interest, by a private creditor. Normally such savings would be spread over the various kinds of investments, so that, in the rare cases where a savings bank crashed or a property was not sufficient to cover a mortgage debt, there was no total disaster. The depreciation of the mark, however, meant total loss across the entire portfolio.

Besides the *rentiers*, who relied entirely for their income on revenues of this kind, the middle classes included a large group of people who were able to supplement their earnings from such sources. These additional incomes and the possession of the capital from which they stemmed were of the utmost importance for the recipients' standard of living and rôle in the life of the nation, for reasons which, if not unique, were characteristic of German society. This category comprised mainly civil servants of all kinds, judges, magistrates, teachers of all grades, scholars and academics, and to some degree, the members of the professions. They were pillars of society, whose contributions to all that was best in Germany, to science, scholarship, research, standards of education and intellectual life in general, the quality of justice and of public administration, were immense. Professional soldiers, the officers of Imperial Germany in particular, largely shared the economic circumstances of these groups. Yet their social standing, the prestige attached to the wearers of the "King's túnic", was such that it does not seem accurate to lump them together with the middle class.

What enabled them all to play their part so well was, to some considerable degree at least, due to the "cushioning" provided by their "unearned" incomes, and, when the collapse of the currency deprived them of it, the ensuing penury not only impaired their performance, but had an impact on their attitude towards the community and the State which they had served so well.

It was a fact of German life that the material rewards for public service — that is to say, for the members of the classes mentioned above — were meagre. The salaries of public servants, even in the higher ranks, were modest and hardly commensurate with the standard of life they were expected to maintain. Those who pursued a professional career (research in science, the arts, medicine and the like) often had to fend for themselves for years before receiving any sort of living wage at all.

Germany before the Great War was, of course, a prosperous country, getting richer all the time; and, for the individual, either inherited wealth or subsidies from the family fortune in one form or another offered one way of solving the problem of finances. The other way was to marry money. It was, indeed, the familiar story of the impoverished European aristocrat gilding his escutcheon by marrying the Dollar Princess, the difference being that there were many more German civil servants, doctors, judges and the like living precariously than there were impoverished aristocrats, and the dowries their brides brought with them did not amount to millions of dollars, but still to quite a comfortable few thousand marks. So the *Herr Professor,* or *Regierungsrat* or *Privatdocent* married the rich butcher's daughter and received perhaps a block of flats or a wad of government securities complete with a pair of scissors to cut the interest-bearing "coupons". It was a good bargain for both sides.

For if the professional man's work was not worth very

much in hard cash, the implicit privileges and status symbols that State and society accorded him were considerable. The official or professional qualifications displayed on his visiting card, the form by which he was addressed, the Court uniform the "Royal Secondary Schoolteacher" was entitled to wear on special occasions, as well as the assurance of honours and titles to come — the Order of the Red Eagle Third Class, the titles of *Geheimrat, Wirklicher Geheimrat,* perhaps even "Excellency" — were potentially tangible assets.

Much fun has been made of the German habit of addressing a wife by her husband's title or professional qualification — the famous *Frau Doctor,* for instance — but there was a solid social and economic reality behind this tinsel.

It was an unfortunate coincidence that, while the Inflation undermined the economic foundation of these classes, the Constitution of the Weimar Republic abolished titles and other honours and so hurt their pride and diminished, in their view at least, their ties and identification with the existing order. The two factors combined in alienating these classes from the democratic régime, with dire consequences for the future.

It is difficult to assess with any accuracy the material benefits that these classes actually obtained from their extra incomes: they certainly varied from modest sums to very large ones. But, whatever their extent, they exerted a marked influence on their material style of living, on their social and intellectual life, on the way they fashioned their careers and, last but not least, on the educational and other advantages they were able to provide for their children. All this combined to fashion their ideas and attitudes as citizens, and it was only logical that these ideas and attitudes were affected by the

127

revolutionary changes in their circumstances that the Inflation set in motion.

The ability to entertain more or less lavishly, the annual cure in fashionable spas, the privileges of elegant attire and comfortable, often luxurious, accommodation could be attained by these sections of the middle classes only through their private means. The greater latitude in their finances enabled them to play a prominent part in social and political life, on both a local and a national scale. It was they that supported the arts, bought the books, filled the concert halls, and formed an integral part of the audiences in the innumerable theatres and opera houses, which were the pride and, indeed, one of the hallmarks of German civilisation. Without them, the country's intellectual and cultural life and achievements would have been much poorer. German scholarship was financed to some extent from these resources. Take, for instance, the history of art — *Kunstgeschichte* — a branch of scholarship that Germany was pioneering. Now, the typical *Kunsthistoriker* was a rich young man who would dedicate years of study and large sums of money to the pursuit of learning and research, a truly profitless profession, without any payment for his labours until he achieved his *magnum opus* and was perhaps rewarded by a professorship or similar appointment. That species was killed by the Inflation. The income from his, or his father's, investments had gone the way of all paper marks; there was no money for books or learned journals — the tools of his trade — not even enough money to keep body and soul together.

Perhaps the most disturbing aspect of the inflationary losses of the middle class concerned the education of their children and the mentality of these young people themselves.

Education both secondary and higher in the German Reich was not free, but school and university fees were not high, and those for secondary education, given the virtual non-existence of the boarding school, no great problem. However, for university students, who would be unlikely to live at home, scholarships and other grants were extremely rare, so that as a rule the family had to provide the monthly cheque for the student's upkeep. Generally speaking, the ambition of the parents was to give their offspring a good time as well as the opportunity to widen his horizon — but all this cost money. Traditionally, the money earmarked for this purpose came from the doomed securities; the meagre salary of a judge or teacher would not have been sufficient to keep the son in the style in which he and his parents wanted him to live.

Some indication of the deterioration of the traditional comfortable life-style of the German student is given by the experience of Mrs Ehrhardt's husband when he was a student at Bonn University. He was the son of a surgeon in Königsberg in the east of Germany. So hard up was he, that when his vacations began he actually walked across much of western Germany because he could not afford the full fare home. Later on, when he was studying at Berlin University, he had to go without lunch and used to pass the time attending lectures on Swahili, which happened to be given during the lunch hour.

The way in which the unfortunate middle-class victims of the Inflation were expropriated was frighteningly simple. We have the testimony of Hildegard Schlegel, whose father died leaving a life insurance policy intended to provide for the family and the education of the daughter. The proceeds of the insurance, eroded by the Inflation, were just sufficient to buy one loaf of bread, and young Hildegard, robbed of the prospect of continuing her education, had to take a job in a bank (and try her hand at the stock market).

The Ehrhardt family suffered in the same way:

> My father had taken out endowment insurance for his three elder children — the youngest was five weeks old when he died of pneumonia and no provision was made for her. The insurance was calculated to cover my brothers' university education and I was to have a similar amount. When my eldest brother got his money it was just sufficient to buy a bicycle. When the second got his, he could just buy a pair of boots. When my turn came I got nothing.

No provisions for the future made by prudent heads of families in the normal way could survive the erosions of inflation. W.G. relates,

> My father had sold his business during the war together with all the real-estate property he owned, and retired from active business. He was, by middle-class standards, a rich man and intended to live as a *rentier* on the proceeds of his investments. These were mainly life-insurance policies, fixed-value securities, among them a lot of war loan, and the biggest single item was a mortgage on a large agricultural estate of 300,000 marks, whose yield of 15,000 marks per annum would have provided a very good income. All this depreciated, of course, to zero — my father managed to keep his head above water by resuming some work. The impact on my own life was dramatic. Once upon a time I had dreamed of a

glamorous student existence *à la* old Heidelberg as the birthright of a rich man's son. The reality, as I have described, was very different: even by early 1922 that fabulous income from the big mortgage was not much more than was necessary to maintain me for a couple of terms in very reduced circumstances. My friend and fellow-student, Friedrich W., shared my mode of living. His father, a doctor, had also been the owner of a very valuable property and therefore very well off. He had sold his property for depreciating paper marks, and he was one of those professional men whose income had not kept in step with the Inflation. So Friedrich and I took our meals together in the Mensa Academica and I never saw the inside of the alluring taverns and cafés of our university town, Freiburg.

The case of Friedrich W.'s father, who sold his property for paper marks, is typical of one category of inflation losers. It is a paradoxical case and needs some explanation.

Property in land, by definition, was a *Sachwert,* a real value, and its ownership should have been the perfect hedge against inflation. In principle it was; and, indeed, the owners of property were, as the experience of the vast majority of them confirms, typical Inflation *profiteers.* For properties urban and rural, agricultural, industrial and residential, were heavily mortgaged — many, as the saying went, "up to the chimney pots". These mortgage debts were, of course, for a fixed number of paper marks, and, as we have seen, the mortgagee's loss and ruin were the mortgagor's gain and bonanza.

There was one kind of property that was an exception to the rule: the apartment building, the block of flats let out for rent, including tenement houses and slum or semi-slum property. The owners of these buildings, which were usually mortgaged like other property, were on the one hand gaining on the swings of inflation as their debts vanished, but on the other hand losing on the roundabouts of the rent acts and the confusion of the Inflation era. And many of them lost heavily.

The Germans were a nation of flat-dwellers, rather than house-owners. The ownership and occupation of a house or villa was normally the privilege of the rich, and they were exempt from the peculiar tribulations of the owners of property for letting. As the law, with negligible exceptions, did not permit ownership of parts of a building, living in a flat meant, to all intents and purposes, renting it. Blocks of flats were a popular investment, the rents providing the owner with an income. The size and value of a property naturally varied very much. Some rich people even owned several of them. But a typical case was, perhaps, a four-storey building, possibly with a couple of shops on the ground floor and six or eight flats above, one of which might be occupied by the owner himself. Its price in the estate market was perhaps in the 100,000–200,000 marks range and the net income to the owner, dependent of course on the extent of the mortgage charges, would be a few thousand marks a year, in itself sufficient to provide a reasonable living. Bricks and mortar were by definition a safe investment. The rental income was on the whole sound, the law and the usual terms of contract giving the landlord rather stringent (not always ideally fair) rights *vis-à-vis* the tenant.

The relationship between landlord and tenant and the financial conditions of the former were thrown into confusion by the twin legacies of the war: inflation and rent control.

Inflation put paid to the landlord's mortgage liabilities, in both capital and interest, thus presenting him with a huge profit and leaving him with his bricks and mortar, that paragon of a *Sachwert,* unencumbered by debts. This worked to perfection for the owner of agricultural land or industrial premises, but for the owner of rented residential property it was by no means so simple. Of course he had a *Sachwert* in his hands and, if he were able to hold on to it and to survive until currency stability returned, his property operated as a more or less successful hedge against inflation. But that was an enormous IF, and tenacity, foresight and a good deal of willingness to make sacrifices were the essential prerequisites for success. For the almost total shortfall of rents, which was only partially compensated by the cessation of his mortgage liabilities, left him without the income on which he relied. Any chance of getting rid of a tenant and utilising the latter's premises to some advantage was nullified by the security of tenure which the law granted. If ever there was an illustration of the principle that inflation is a redistribution of wealth, here it was in the form of the transfer, from the owner to the tenant, of the benefits deriving from property. The tenant's advantage — the enjoyment of virtual freedom from paying rent for his flat — was in its turn partially lost to him. The benefit went to his employer, who used the fact of free rent to keep his wages low. But the landlord's tribulations did not end with his loss of income; he remained basically responsible for the upkeep of the property, and such expenses were only marginally reduced by the Inflation. The accumulated neglect of the wartime years and the effect of one ugly phenomenon of the Inflation, namely the theft of such

Sachwerte as stair carpets, door-handles, metal fixtures of all descriptions, electric light bulbs — in short, anything that could be extracted from a building by a desperate thief — added to the dilapidation of the property and to the landlord's impotence to prevent the property's falling into complete disrepair. To these material factors were added the psychological ones of constant worry and discontent, aggravated by resentment of the tenants, who, in the view of the landlords, became more and more "uppish". Even if the owner were not actually forced to sell out there were understandable motives for getting rid of what had become a burden.

Moreover, there were positive inducements to do so.

For many people with stacks of paper money at their disposal, and particularly for foreigners, who, with their powerful foreign currency, could buy marks so cheaply, these buildings still remained valuable *Sachwerte* worth acquiring — which indeed they were for anybody not interested in any income from them or in their shocking state of repair. It should be remembered that in 1922 and the first months of 1923 prices in Germany were comparatively low, for reasons already explained. As for blocks of flats, the price level was further depressed by the traditional rule that an investment lost its value when the yield from it had sunk to the point of non-existence. Thus, a would-be purchaser was in a position to offer sums in paper money which dazzled the unfortunate owners and constituted a well-nigh irresistible lure, especially in 1922, when the true nature of the Inflation was not yet common knowledge. Many, apart from those who were actually forced to do so by their circumstances, were tempted to sell; and with the millions and milliards they received in cash they joined the masses who held paper marks or paper securities, and shared in their fate

— complete penury. Always, of course, with the exception of a few clever ones.

The number of such transactions was very large, much larger than before the war (and, incidentally, lawyers, who suffered very much from the Inflation, found themselves somewhat compensated by the benefits they received from the increased conveyancing practice). It was estimated that one third of all apartment buildings in Berlin changed hands during this period, and that the total value of Germany's urban property sold to foreigners amounted to 4 milliard gold marks. But later a special situation arose when some of these winners lost their gains and the losers somehow recouped their losses. It was a freak, but a freak that sheds some light on the dark recesses of the Inflation, and this seems the place to describe it briefly. It has made legal history under the name of the "black sale cases".

The individual prices obtained in these transactions were, of course, fabulous: millions and more of paper marks — in numerical terms, multiples of the pre-war gold mark values (hardly likely to exceed a few hundred thousand marks each) of properties of this sort. A capital gains tax existed in Germany. This tax was progressive and the rates of tax in the upper grades were very high. The principle "mark equals mark" also applied in this field, so that the gain was calculated on the difference between the number of marks for which the property had been bought and the number of marks for which it was sold — regardless of the real intrinsic value in gold of the price of acquisition and the price of the sale. In this way, large sums of paper marks became subject to tax as gains, although in fact the selling price represented a real loss. This problem has also been widely discussed in the context of capital gains tax in an inflation-ridden

135

Britain. (A letter to *The Times* of 13th November 1973 complains, "It is, I believe, high time that a severe injustice is . . . corrected. I refer, of course, to the fact that no account is taken in calculating a capital gain of the fall in the value of the pound . . .")

Understandably, given the circumstances in Germany, the seller did not want to pay a considerable proportion of what was in reality a meagre price to the tax collector, and often the purchaser co-operated with him. This was done by handing over part of the purchase money in cash, black money over the counter, only the relatively small balance appearing in the sales document submitted to the tax authorities for assessment. Everybody was happy until, years later, a test case was brought by one of the "black sellers" and the German Supreme Court decided that such a contract was null and void. This is not the place to go into the legal and ethical niceties of the decision. The outcome was that some of the Inflation losers, at any rate, got back their *Sachwerte,* and the "black buyers" lost their Inflation profit.

In one of the most moving works of literature to take its theme from the Inflation, a short story by Stefan Zweig called *Die unsichtbare Sammlung* ("The Invisible Collection"), an art dealer relates his meeting with an impoverished civil servant, now on pension. The narrator, desperately trying to replenish his stocks, which the *nouveaux riches* of the Inflation are buying up wildly as *Sachwerte,* has discovered that the old man has been a client of his firm for decades, buying old prints and etchings, and thinks that he might find in him a willing seller. But the collector's family, hard hit by inflation, their pension having dwindled to starvation level, have been forced to sell practically all the precious works of art, substituting blank sheets of paper for them (the old

136

gentleman had been blind for many years, which enabled them to do this without his knowing about it). The story reaches its climax as the old man proudly displays his invisible collection to the visitor, describing the sketches one by one and convinced that the fulfilment of his life-long ambition is there for all to see.

Unlike the hero of Zweig's story, the impoverished middle class knew only too well what had happened to them, knew that they were poor and *déclassé*; they were hurt and resentful, and this changed them. For, when the Inflation was over, the social structure of Germany was found to have been profoundly altered: the steady middle class had been proletarianised.

Opinions vary on both the extent to which the middle class suffered and the effect this suffering produced. An extremist view, heard at the time, was that these people were capitalist parasites on whom not too much pity should be wasted; in any case they were rich, and somebody had to pay for the economic consequences of the war. Moreover, it is pointed out that the increase of business activity under the stimulus of the Inflation offered many opportunities to those whose patrimony had been eroded by the depreciation of the mark. People who had been living in retirement set up in business, perhaps with some little capital they had salvaged from the wreck of their bonds and securities; public servants, both those retired and those still in office, but in reduced circumstances on account of their poor remuneration and the loss of private income, obtained employment in the booming branches of the private sector of the economy. (Incidentally this shift of employees from the public into the more remunerative private sectors is a familiar phenomenon in contemporary inflation, too.)

No doubt many took such evasive action and the

transition proved successful, beneficial and satisfying to them; but others were barred from doing so by lack of flexibility or because their special talents and qualifications were not in demand — particularly true of higher-grade civil servants. But, for the very old, particularly for the women, there was no hope anywhere. Particularly sad was the plight of those daughters for whom a prudent and loving father had made comfortable provision against the time when his own protection would be removed by death. Unmarried and unskilled in any profession, they became the flotsam of the Inflation, kept alive in the end by the kindness of strangers. At the Quaker relief depot that she ran in Frankfurt, Dorothy Haenkel was moved by the plight of these poor women:

> There were so many old ladies, daughters of really well-known families in Frankfurt — and there was a very fine aristocracy in Frankfurt and, above all, great culture.
>
> One woman asked me to supper one evening. This was the time when you carefully avoided visiting people at meal-times, but I could see that she would be so happy if she could give something instead of just receiving. When I arrived she put down a little dish with two thin slices of the tin of corned beef I'd given her at the depôt and she said, "You see, I didn't need my lunch today so there is enough for both of us." It was quite — sacramental. Of course, I ate it. You had to feel your way — some of them were so delighted to give. One knew they had known very much better days and had been used to giving things.

Another group of women were affected in a very

special way by the sheer momentum that the Inflation gained as the months went by. Again, Dorothy Haenkel has a heartbreaking story to tell:

> A friend of mine was in charge of the office that had to deal with the giving out of salaries, pensions and special grants to the police of the whole district around Frankfurt. This was at the time when the bank notes were showing as many as twelve noughts. She struggled with her task very bravely. One case which came her way was the widow of a policeman who had died early leaving four children. She had been awarded three months of her late husband's salary. My friend worked out the sum with great care, checked it and double-checked it and sent the papers on as required to Wiesbaden. There they were again checked, rubber-stamped and sent back to Frankfurt. By the time all this was done and the money was finally paid out to the widow, the amount she received would only have paid for three boxes of matches.

The status of the "entrepreneurs", into which many of the newly deprived middle class turned themselves, had nothing of the glamour suggested by their grandiloquent title. In fact, they were a sorry lot. They included an army of tiny shopkeepers, who often made a precarious living by selling their heirlooms and the valuables that their even more unfortunate fellow sufferers had been forced to trade in for the daily necessities; but they could not afford to light their premises properly or even give them a fresh coat of paint. Then there were the street-corner dealers engaged in a similar business; the agents and middlemen living on the hot air of the Inflation bubble;

and elderly pensioners, dressed in the shabby fashions of yesteryear, visiting their more fortunate friends and peddling small lots of wine.

> My uncle Gustav [remembers W.G.] had retired at the age of 67 in 1914 from a prosperous business with a comfortable fortune; inflation had reduced him to penury and now, over 70 years old, he had become a small-scale insurance agent earning with his meagre commission too much to die and too little to live on. On his rounds trying to sell insurance and collecting the premiums he used to call regularly at our house — he was an avid reader and he came to borrow our copy of the daily paper which he himself was too poor to buy.

The social revolution originating in the financial distress of the middle classes was perhaps even more in the minds of the people affected than in their material condition. The bitterness and resentment, caused by the actual deprivation as much as by hurt pride and vanity, turned against those who were blamed for the state of affairs: against the government, and the former enemies of Germany; against the Allies for exacting, and against the government for agreeing to pay, reparations; against the people who did well out of the Inflation: speculators, financiers and Jews. All this meant an upsurge of hatred against the democratic régime of the Weimar Republic, resulting in right-wing radicalism, reaction, nationalism, xenophobia and anti-semitism. People had lost their faith in liberalism and the philosophy of moderation, of which Weimar was a symbol, and in despair they turned to extremism.

To what degree their grievances and the resulting

attitudes, with their large admixture of envy and wounded vanity, were justified, and whether the shift to the Right was but an extension of the nationalism and super-patriotism that had been the traditional creed of some sectors of that class are moot points. All that counts is the result. If the erstwhile symbol of stable values, money, had proved to be a chimera, other old values were proving equally illusory; and people were ready to worship new gods in their stead.

Chapter 5

On the Stock Exchange

Every day at a certain hour the central lobby of the local branch of one of the great German banks used to fill with all the bank employees down to the most humble apprentice, eagerly watching a young man frantically talking on the telephone and taking notes. It was summer 1923. The Inflation was moving rapidly to its dizzy climax. The young speaker at the telephone was the *Effektenhändler*, the man in charge of Stock-Exchange business and share dealing, and he was talking to his counterpart in Berlin to hear the latest prices of the dollar and equities. The dapper young man, fashionably attired in a sharp gaberdine suit, was the centre of attention whilst the manager of the branch, a staid, middle-aged gentleman, author of a learned treatise on the legal aspects of bank credit, looked on from the background, soon to disappear shaking his head in wonderment.

When the *Effektenhändler* emerged with the news of the turbulent movement on the Berlin Stock

> Exchange the audience was seized by excitement and every person began to consider the situation, calculating what he had gained or lost, what now to sell or buy and hurrying to place his orders accordingly.

The scene, so vividly recalled by a former bank employee, was repeated all over Germany as the Inflation reached its peak. Bank employees were, of course, well placed to take part in this business, as Hildegard Schlegel, whose story we told in the previous chapter, realised. She took employment in the bank, attracted by the opportunities for playing the market, and indeed she managed to keep her family going out of the proceeds resulting from regularly investing her wages.

Harold Fraser, who worked as a bank clerk in Hamburg, reported to his head office in London on 30th June 1923,

> The majority of the people, finding it quite useless to save money, either use their surplus (at present not much) for purchasing clothes, or else in speculating on the Bourse. They buy shares of industrial companies and in many cases, with quite small capital, are able to realise good profits on selling them. As a rule, however, if a profit is taken, the money is at once put into something else. I can say that, without exaggeration, 90 per cent of the men employed in the Deutsche Bank keep their money (such as it is) in this manner.

Contrast with this the case of another young bank clerk at the time — Robert Berman. Owing to special circumstances, his salary was fixed in pounds sterling. As foreign currency was the ideal incarnation of a "stable value", superior, in principle, to any stocks or shares, he never dreamed of joining in the game of speculating on the Stock Exchange. He drew his salary in driblets only just sufficient to cover his immediate needs and, unable to consume all that was due to him when the next pay-day arrived, he found himself the owner of a surplus of pounds sterling. He was thus that most envied person — a little capitalist in "stable values".

But not only were those people close to the fountain-head of the share business drawn into this speculation fever. Starting slowly in 1919/1920 — when recognition of the true nature of the Inflation gradually began to seep into the consciousness of some people — it extended progressively to all sections of the population from working man to small employer, civil servant, magistrate, university professor and *rentier*. It was for the masses simply a necessity, a means of self-defence against the ravages of inflation and a way of, economically speaking, keeping one's head above water. There were also, of course, the lions of the stock market, the really big operators who exploited the turbulence and turned it into a source of enormous profits. They were the aggressors in the inflation war, quite different from the army of little men on the defensive in a struggle for survival.

This was a new phenomenon for Germany. There had always been, of course, a huge stock-exchange business, and dealing in the stocks and shares of the numberless companies of that rich and growing industrial country; but such activity was mainly confined to the rich or very rich, to big business and professional operators. The ordinary man in the street, the small and not-so-small saver, would regard the *Börseaner,* the man who played the market, as something of an adventurer, his profits as somewhat suspect, if not malodorous — and anyhow it was too risky and nerve-racking for his taste. If you want to eat well, play the market; but if you want to sleep well, so the saying went, keep away from stocks and shares and invest your money in mortgages, bonds, fixed-interest securities, and so on, and not only would your money be safe, you would also know exactly the income you would obtain from such investments.

But these people saw the actual value of their incomes dwindle with the progressive devaluation of the mark. The value of the capital itself, expressed in paper marks, also dwindled, because a mark always remained a mark whatever its purchasing power. So, as the notion spread about how easy it was to make money on the Stock Exchange, more and more people jumped on the bandwagon of speculators. Admittedly, millions were too timid, impractical or old-fashioned to do so, and for the majority of them their reluctance only precipitated their financial ruin. But those who did participate did so with great élan and tenacity. In his *Wandering Scholar,* Professor Bonn tells the story of a university teacher who was regularly late for his eleven o'clock lecture because he had to rush to the telephone to give instructions before the Stock Exchange opened; later, as the clock struck twelve, he had to rush back to the telephone to give new orders. The backwoodsmen in Germany's agricultural districts, far away from the financial centres, all had telephones installed in order to keep in touch, minute by minute, with developments at the Stock Exchange and to arrange their deals. A young doctor sold his bicycle, to the great distress of his friends who relied on borrowing it, to get money for investment in the shares of an obscure publishing house, and so on.

Were these people speculators aiming at a quick profit

to pay for the week's groceries or a riotous night in a night club — or were they investors, seeking a hoard of values as a safe haven for their savings, which, hopefully, would give them a regular return? Today, when even somebody who plays the football pools is styled an "investor", the difference between the two is blurred, and so it was, in an even more bewildering way, during the German Inflation.

The basic idea was that the ownership of a share (unlike that of a title deed or a mortgage, or any fixed-sum security, which represented only the sum of money printed on it) imparted a share in the actual bricks and mortar, property and machinery — in brief, in all the assets — of the company and was therefore a "real", not a paper, value. The value of the share would move with the value of the underlying assets: that is to say, upwards, if the currency depreciated. (It should be noted in passing that occasionally, and with some success, speculators turned their attention even to fixed-money securities. But these were special situations as, for instance, in the case of a State Colonial Loan, the buyers of which deluded themselves into thinking that the new masters of Germany's lost colonies would honour the debt.)

The idea is eminently plausible and one has only to look at the advertisements that, in modern inflationary times, invite the public to acquire unit trusts, property bonds, managed-income bonds and so forth as a hedge against inflation to see that the idea is very much alive. These modern instruments for the defence against inflation, representing as they do a wide spread of shares of every description and a variety of other assets, are of course well thought out, thanks to the financial expertise of those who create them.

The Great Inflation

The crass laymen who, in the Germany of the nineteen-twenties, plunged into the share markets were less fortunate than their present counterparts. They had to rely on some casual information (they did their business usually through the bank, not using the services of an individual broker) or rumour and mere guesswork. In the feverish economic climate of the time, many bogus companies whose name promised some "material" basis (Oder Sand was the name of one of them) found eager buyers for their shares. Yet, even though such shares were worthless as an investment, as long as they were still in the market and followed its movements, they were good enough for the purposes of mere speculation.

But if one asks the question whether, all shares taken together, they remained unaffected by the depreciation of the currency and rose automatically in unison with the dollar, the answer is "no". The relationship varied very much over the Inflation years; sometimes the share prices kept pace with the dollar rate, sometimes went ahead of it, and sometimes fell sharply back.

Two examples will suffice to show how illusory the theory was that shares in a company would reflect in their value that of the assets of the company itself. It is to be admitted, however, that the figures quoted are exceptional, reflecting a particularly sharp rise in the dollar rate and the cost of living index.

In November 1922 the capitalisation of the Daimler Motor Works — the sum total of the value of its shares based on the Stock-Exchange quotation — was 980 million paper marks. At that time the average price of a Daimler car was 3 million marks. So the Stock Exchange attributed a value equivalent to that of 327 cars to the Daimler capital, made up as it was of three great factories, an extensive area of land, its reserves and its liquid capital, and its commercial organisation developed in Germany and abroad. Similarly, the capitalisation of the big company that owned the 16 department stores of Tietz equalled the price of 16,000 men's suits.

This sort of undervaluation was by no means restricted to isolated cases, and only the fact that the effective control of such companies was in the hands of shareholders with plural votes prevented asset-strippers and others from getting possession of the firm.

No wonder that when, in the early days of December 1922, and in response to the enormous increase in business transacted, a fourth room was added to the premises of the Berlin Stock Exchange, the wits quipped, "The funeral cortège of the Stock-Exchange boom will leave from the new fourth room of the Bourse." Yet Stock-Exchange business roared on for another year at an ever-accelerating pace.

The simple explanation of the divergence of share prices and money values is, of course, the fact that share prices are subject not only to the vagaries of currency depreciation, but to other forces as well. That is true today; in the Germany of the Inflation it was complicated by the fact that the depreciation of the mark was closely linked to the dollar rate, and the fact that the movements of foreign exchange played a dominant rôle in the German economy as a whole, being reflected increasingly closely in the prices of goods and the cost of living.

The prices of shares were, of course, basically influenced by the demand for them: the greater the demand the higher the price. But the demand depended on a variety of circumstances, such as the amount of money available (either the sum total of money in circulation or the amount apportioned by the buying public to the purchase of shares in preference to other

means of investment), political considerations and the
confidence in the German economy, or just the moods
and whims of the public. The curious fact is, that even
adverse economic conditions might, in certain circumstances, produce a rising stock market. This happened in
the last months of the Inflation, when Germany found
herself in a grave crisis, faced with stagnation of
economic activity, unemployment and a desperate
shortage of goods, and yet, from July to the beginning of
November 1923, the Stock Exchange experienced an
unprecedented boom. A financial paper commented at
the time, "There have been extraordinary rises in the
quotations of all shares, the chief cause being the
catastrophic change in the economic situation." It was
surely just a manifestation of the panic that had seized
the people in the chaotic conditions of the time that they
frantically strove to lay their hands on anything that
might give them the chance of rescuing something out of
the expected national bankruptcy.

The aim of the share-buying multitude was therefore
to preserve their money, be it capital or income, from the
ravages of the Inflation. For some people this took the
form of short-term, often day-to-day speculation for a
quick profit, with which to counteract as far as possible
the rising cost of living. In this they followed the
legendary advice of a member of the Rothschild family,
who when asked how to succeed on the Stock Exchange,
said, "The thing is simple — act on the Stock Exchange
the same way as when taking a cold bath: jump in
quickly and get out quickly." Others intended to
"invest"; that is to say, to use the shares as an
inflation-proof store of value, a "real value". The usual
purpose of an investment, namely to give the investor a
return in the form of dividends, was, at the time of the

German Inflation, a minor consideration. Investors usually went, as the modern saying goes, for growth, not for income; that the growth was largely imaginary, a paper profit, hardly ever dawned on them.

For dividend payments, in general, were derisory. In December 1922 the *Industrie- und Handelszeitung* reported that the average yield for a large number of industrial shares amounted to a quarter per cent. This "conservative" dividend policy was widely praised in industrial circles as "prudent" and necessary in order to reinforce continuously the internal structure of the firm, and the profits were largely used for re-investment within the enterprise. Indeed, company directors treated their shareholders in a rather cavalier manner. Professor Bonn quotes a leading banker presiding over a shareholders' meeting as saying, "Why should I throw my good money away for the benefit of people I don't know?", when asked by a shareholder why the company did not pay higher dividends. But few were deterred by such attitudes.

How, then, did buyers of shares fare during the Inflation? Did the holding of shares afford a hedge against inflation?

If one inquires whether a person who owned shares before the war benefited if he held on to them through the Inflation years until after the stabilisation of the mark in 1923, the answer is that he did not. By the end of 1923, share prices in comparison with the cost of living index were worth only about one sixth of what they had been before 1913. That is to say, the persistent long-term shareholder had preserved in real value only a fraction of his pre-war fortune — certainly better than losing everything, as did many bond holders and the like — but nevertheless a considerable loss.

The Great Inflation

But this rather crude calculation leaves out of account the fact that share prices, for reasons that will be explained later, fluctuated very much. In the period just after the end of the war in 1918, share prices were already very depressed, and later they took periodical plunges downward as on, for instance, the famous "Black Thursday" of 1st December 1921 and other "black" days in May 1922, February 1923, and on 5th November 1923. The big battalions of Stock-Exchange operators entered the field only after 1919, at a time when shares were already cheap, and they had similar opportunities for buying cheaply during the successive bear markets and thus enjoyed a more favourable starting point in the struggle for the preservation of their money. Some of these hundreds of thousands of ordinary middle-class people of limited means — the *rentiers*, small employers, professional men — who sought an economic haven on the Stock Exchange were quite successful "investors". They bought shares in first-class enterprises at a time when their price was depressed through the vicissitudes of the Inflation and, through holding on to them until the more prosperous years of the middle twenties, when a bull market developed, were able to emerge from the Inflation with a goodly nest-egg.

This happened in the case of a civil servant who, by promptly and regularly using part of his salary to buy shares in a big, very prosperous enterprise in the drink industry, found himself in 1927 possessed of a sizable fortune. (In this connection it should be remembered that for a brief period in 1923 civil-service employees were, through a freak, relatively well off, as their salary was made up over and over again to keep pace with the daily changes in the dollar index.)

Somewhat different was the position of those

152

speculators, and they were the great majority, who, by gambling on the Stock Exchange, aimed at making quick paper profits by constant buying and selling, stretching their paper-mark assets or supplementing their inadequate incomes with their profits in order just to keep alive. By doing this many people who otherwise would have starved managed to eat and to survive though they were left penniless afterwards. It was a case of poverty postponed, as the following example illustrates.

Take the case of Mrs A., widowed in 1921 and left by her husband a life insurance of 50,000 marks. When paid out, the money was, of course, grossly devalued, but it was still worth, say, 5,000 gold marks. Instead of choosing the traditional investment in fixed-interest securities, destined to become worthless through inflation, somebody helped her to use the money for share dealings. There was always — apart from some interruptions — a paper profit accruing, and Mrs A. realised this in order to live, since the shares yielded her very little income. In this way, the actual intrinsic value of her share holdings gradually diminished, but though in the end she had spent the lot, she was much better off than she would have been with 50,000 paper marks in bonds.

In a similar way, lawyer F.G. would immediately buy shares whenever he had a windfall, such as a big fee from the conveyance of a large enterprise. (Income from litigation was very small, since people were naturally reluctant to fight in the courts for sums of money that melted away as the court case went on.) He would gradually sell off these shares at increasing paper values, in order to provide himself with the money he needed for the necessities of life.

Bank clerk L.K. did much better; he was better informed and picked his shares with greater discrimination, selecting those that would more than make good the depreciation of the paper mark, and not only make him enough profit to live on, but also leave him enough over to buy gold watches. Gold watches were an even better "value" than shares; he became rich.

As we have said, shares moved rather erratically, sometimes in step with the dollar, thereby providing a real hedge against inflation, and sometimes not. The reasons for these discrepancies are illuminating and they are set out here in brief and simplified form.

When, around 1920, the stock market began to play a major rôle as a hoped-for defence against inflation, share prices on the whole followed the price of the dollar, as they continued to do until December 1921. The dollar had become the popular yardstick for real values and, in the same way as shares in a company were considered to represent the actual assets of that company, it was only logical that the dollar and shares, being two representatives of the same thing, should be considered as more or less equivalent. So strong was the public belief in this rule, that when such events as the loss to Germany of part of Upper Silesia (under the terms of the Treaty of Versailles) drove the dollar rate up, shares followed suit instead of going down, as would have been the natural reaction to bad news, political and economic. Thus, for that period, shares were a good hedge against inflation.

In 1922 the picture changed drastically. First slowly, then with increasing speed, the rate of the dollar overtook the price of shares; between January and December the dollar rate increased 40 times, share prices only 12. Shares had become an extremely poor hedge against inflation. The sudden fall of share prices on 1st December 1921 had made people change their ideas on shares as direct and accurate representatives of real value.

Moreover, money was short. The Report of the Reichsbank for 1922 speaks of scarcity of money and capital, and shows that in the beginning of 1922 the note circulation rose only from 113,000 million to 169,000 million, a very modest increase compared to the rise at other times. As a result, the holders of the available money decided that there were more attractive ways of investing it, and the stock market suffered.

This is a perfectly normal development and varies according to what in particular catches the fancy of the investing public or the speculators. In the summer of 1973, for instance, the London stock market languished and share prices were not even boosted by spectacular rises in the profits of individual companies. This was largely because the prices of commodities like metals, grain and cocoa had, under the impact of intense speculative activity, appreciated fantastically, reaching unprecedented heights. "The commodity markets", *The Economist* of 11th August 1973 commented, "have been steadily siphoning off money from Wall Street and London."

What attracted money away from the share market in 1922 was foreign currency, represented by the dollar, which was, in the public mind, the yardstick of all values. Having received its most dramatic stimulus from the murder of the Foreign Minister, Rathenau, and the developments of the reparations problem in summer 1922, the dollar rose relentlessly against the mark, increasing its value about seven times between July and October. At the same time, confirming the public's opinion that the dollar was the real yardstick, internal prices and the cost of living were keeping much more in step with the dollar than ever before. Over the period from July to October, the cost of living increased about

155

five times while the price of shares just about doubled. The fact that the prices of shares were also determined by a failing confidence, both inside Germany and abroad, in Germany's economic future is beside the point. Suffice it to say that those who were able to buy dollars were beating the inflationary rise in prices (driven up also by the increasing urge to buy "real values" in kind), whilst investors in shares fell considerably behind. The circulation of paper marks, which caused all these inflationary pressures, rose between June and December from about 40,000 million to over 150,000 million marks' worth.

Late in 1922 the picture changed again, indeed was reversed. In order to prevent "the manipulation of dishonest elements", to quote the Reichsbank's Report for 1922, "and to counteract the widespread desire to use foreign currency as an investment", the government issued, on 12th October 1922, a "drastic decree against speculation in foreign currency", which severely controlled all transactions in foreign exchange.

In the course of 1923, legislation to control foreign currency was reinforced by a number of government decrees. In theory, at least, this made it impossible to hold or acquire any foreign currency without special authorisation. The law authorised drastic interference with the freedom of the individual, including the seizure of foreign currencies wherever they were found, the search of private and public premises and the opening of letters.

As it was no longer possible to use paper marks, the circulation of which was now increasing rapidly, to buy dollars, these paper marks again found their way into the Stock Exchange. So frantic was the onslaught that share prices not only kept in step with the rise of the dollar, but even overtook it substantially.

At the beginning of November 1923, the rise in share prices had reached such a point that the share index in gold briefly surpassed the pre-war index. This was a freak, and the share index soon fell again. But the following hypothesis throws some light on the complexities of the Inflation: if, just before that black November day in 1923, a pre-war shareholder had been able to sell out and invest the paper-mark proceeds immediately in dollars or other "stable values", he would have emerged from the Inflation with his investment not only intact but also increased.

Soon the bubble burst; for after the stabilisation of the currency there was neither need nor opportunity for the masses to rush to seek salvation in the stock markets. Bank offices ceased to be the setting for scenes such as those described at the beginning of this chapter; indeed the banks, through which all this business had been conducted and which had expanded for this reason, began to shrink and this shrinking reflected better than anything else the end of the speculation fever.

As early as 26th January 1924, a couple of months after the stabilisation, Harold Fraser reported, "The banking industry is at present engaged in considerable discharges. On the 1st January the Dresdner Bank discharged 20 per cent of its employees and the Deutsche Bank, it is said, will take exactly the same step on 1st April."

The number of holders of current accounts with the German "big four" banks had reached in 1923 the figure of about 2,500,000 (five times as many as before the war); but in 1924 it had sunk to fewer than 650,000 and the number of employees had fallen by half.

The calm that reigned in the bank offices after

stabilisation reflected the change that had taken place at the Stock Exchange. The Berlin Bourse, where in 1922 business had become so frantic that the number of persons attending it had doubled in comparison with 1913, and which had to remain closed three days a week to catch up with the enormous volume of business, rapidly returned to more normal conditions and, within weeks, many hundreds ceased to attend.

Was this great Stock Exchange bubble an unmitigated social evil? The answer seems to be that it was so only in part.

"From a social point of view," notes a financial journalist writing at the height of the Inflation, "it was a blessing for those particularly hard hit by the inflation, the *rentiers* and the like, because it enabled them to stretch out their assets, which the currency collapse had condemned them to eat up, for long periods." But the phenomenon also had socially deplorable consequences. There were speculators in privileged positions. In his article the writer singles out for censure the employees in certain enterprises and coins a special word — *Angestelltenspekulation* — the speculation that the clerks undertook for those who spent their easy pickings on luxuries and ostentatious high living in a socially objectionable manner.

Finally, there were those large-scale speculators: irresponsible individuals who by more or less unscrupulous means succeeded in building up large fortunes at the expense of the common weal.

Chapter 6

Counter-Attack

The fight against the Inflation and the corrosion of the German currency was conducted on two different levels and with tactics that varied according to the exigencies of the moment.

On the one hand, the men responsible for the country's political and economic destinies recognised their duty to try to save the mark from collapse, to stem the flood of paper disgorged by the printing presses, and to stabilise the currency. They acted accordingly throughout the years of the Inflation, but their actions were determined by their reading of the situation. As they saw the root cause of their country's financial disarray in Germany's external indebtedness, they gave priority to seeking relief from that crushing burden. That, in their own view, was the fundamental precondition for putting their own house in order. Yet they did also take a variety of direct measures to put their internal finances on a more solid basis. But as their efforts in the international field did not have the desired success, these measures tended to be half-hearted and vitiated by the official view that, with the international scene as it was, little could be done to bring the Inflation under control. So the German paper mark drifted to its death.

On the other hand, the German people as individuals, from the ordinary man to the leader of industry, gradually came to resign themselves to the depreciation of the money as a fact of life and to try to defeat inflation simply by avoiding its harmful consequences; to keep afloat on the tidal wave and let their fellow men drown in it. The result was, in the words of one of the directors of the Reichsbank during that era, "an unbridled struggle to push the risk of depreciation on to somebody else, a free-for-all of everybody against everybody else".

Every defensive act of this kind by its very nature made inflation worse, and it is ironic that the Reichsbank itself joined in that game; its way of coping with the shrinking value of money in circulation was just to print more of the stuff and pour it out.

In their diverse attempts to consolidate the finances of the Reich and to stabilise the currency, the German authorities were under pressure not only from democratic and progressive circles within Germany, but also from the Allies, who considered such measures as an essential prerequisite for the payment of reparations. The French, who had been the main sufferers during the war and were the most eager to obtain redress, were in the forefront; and the more nationalist and hard-line the French government of the day, the more insistent it was that Germany must pay, that it was capable of paying because the German economy was doing well and had earned and hoarded sufficient foreign currency for the purpose. It accused the German government of intentionally omitting to mobilise this wealth by drastic taxation and other harsh fiscal measures, and deliberately creating

160

chaotic financial and monetary conditions; that is, pretending to be bankrupt in order to evade its obligations.

The German leadership, for its part, was hampered in its endeavours, such as they were, not only by its conviction that all efforts were futile in the absence of a reparations settlement, but also by pressure from big business, industry and the land-owning classes. These groups were motivated in their resistance by a selfish, but strictly practical, desire to pay as little tax as possible, and a wish to avoid, for political reasons, contributing any more than was necessary to the well-being of the democratic State, which they detested, and their former enemies, whom they equally detested. They also feared that stabilisation of the mark would endanger their inflation-engendered prosperity. Their attitudes went a long way to lend credence to the French point of view. It was more than mere coincidence that stabilisation finally took place when the representatives of German high finance, for reasons of their own, ceased to oppose any moves for rescuing the German currency.

Thus the entire course of the Inflation and the official fight against it is punctuated by events in which fiscal, financial, monetary and diplomatic actions intermingle. They may be summarised as follows:

— government fiscal measures, aimed at covering public expenditure and balancing the budget;
— raising internal loans, aimed at consolidating the floating debt, skimming off purchasing power and providing means to cover external liabilities;
— raising external loans, aimed at obtaining foreign currency for the discharge of external liabilities;
— international agreements, to define, reduce or delay reparations debts;

— foreign exchange controls, aimed at making foreign currency available for the needs of the government;
— support of the mark by purchasing marks for foreign exchange;
— raising the interest rate;
— introduction of inflation-proof means of payment including issue of inflation-proof loans.

The principal fiscal measures taken by the German government in the period prior to stabilisation were tied to particular developments. First there were the measures taken in the period following the defeat in 1918, the armistice, and the emergence of the new republic, at which time the financial disarray of the country was revealed. Later, the London Ultimatum of May 1921 brought home the urgency of finding new means for discharging Germany's liabilities. Finally, the political and economic earthquake of the Ruhr occupation led to more fiscal and financial measures and ultimately made stabilisation imperative.

The purpose of these measures was to obtain income for the Treasury in order to pay for the public debt and ever-rising expenditure; also to skim off purchasing power in the hands of the public, thereby preventing the acquisition of real values — *Sachwerte* — and foreign exchange, which would force up prices and add to the inflationary spiral.

These measures were intermittently successful, but failed in the end because they were too little and too late. Furthermore, they lacked the general support of the nation, and were defeated by the fact that taxes depreciated enormously before they even reached the Treasury. Income from them was never fully sufficient to balance the budget, and there were periods when only fractions of a per cent of public expenditure were covered by the taxes.

The vicissitudes of the government's first fiscal measures, the Erzberger tax reform of 1919–20, were typical. A reform work on the grand scale (it also had the purpose of bringing fiscal legislation into line with the principles of the new constitution), it was complicated and harsh, as it had to be in the disastrous circumstances. Its central part, an emergency levy on property, in particular aroused the wrath of the wealthy and nationalist classes, who denounced it as a devilish device to impoverish the German people and to shift their wealth into the hands of their enemies. Fortified by their moral indignation, they resorted to large-scale tax evasion and managed to transfer as much of their capital as they could into foreign tax-havens. "Capital flight", as this was called, became fashionable and helped to undermine the German currency. Moreover, the teething troubles of the new reform and the need to allow instalment payments of the levy resulted in even longer delays in collection than before, with the result that the money was even more depreciated by the time it was received. The emergency loan, the hoped-for saviour from financial ruin, was a blow that did not hit the nail.

The London Ultimatum of May 1921, with its concrete demands that Germany should not only pay reparations, but also order its own financial and economic condition in such a way as to enable it to pay, brought Germany again face to face with the need to tackle its problems. It was a time when the German economy was prosperous, the rate of unemployment was low, the export trade was booming (enabling big business to tuck away a lot of money abroad), and the balance of trade was improving; only the State claimed to be poverty-stricken. It was by

then realised in Germany that the penury of the State
was produced by the sickness of the mark, which robbed
the State of its real income, as revenue evaporated in the
heat of the Inflation. So a new slogan emerged —
Erfassung der Sachwerte — seizure, or requisition, of
real values. It was an operation advocated by those who
really did have at heart the healthy survival of the
democratic State. The plan was that a part of the
nation's real wealth — land, buildings, industrial plant,
in short *Sachwerte* — unassailable by inflationary
erosion, should be handed over to the Reich. In this way
the government would be enabled not only to fill its
coffers with solid, non-wasting assets and to balance its
budget, but also to discharge its international liabilities.

A bitter controversy ensued between the politicians
and the other interested parties, in particular the
representatives of big business and industry, and it was
against this background that Parliament considered new
tax legislation. The industrialists and nationalists (Hugo
Stinnes among them) cried "Treason!" and repeated
their accusation that transferring private property from
the people to the ownership of the Reich would only
make it an easy prey for the Allies.

In the midst of the tug-of-war those same industrialists, under the banner of the Association of German
Industries, made their own offer of help. They admitted
quite frankly that they had the means needed by the
Reich to pay reparations and bring some order into its
finances. On 28th September 1921 they offered to put at
the disposal of the government the sum of 1 milliard gold
marks; but there were strings attached to this offer. As a
quid pro quo for this rescue operation, they demanded a
greater influence for themselves in the national economy;
the transfer of the most precious economic assets of the

Reich — the nationalised railways — into private hands; and modification in favour of the employers of the social legislation passed by the government (in such matters as the eight-hour working day, collective bargaining and so forth). Faced by violent protests from the trade unions, the government decided not to accept this humiliating offer. (It may be remarked in passing that the industrialists made a very similar offer of financial aid two years later, when conditions had become much more desperate. This offer, too, was rejected.) Thus, the efforts to mobilise the enormous amounts of hard currency at the disposal of Germany's industrialists and businessmen (who were estimated to have accumulated a dollar hoard of 1·5 milliard dollars) came to naught. German industry put its own interests above those of the democratic State.

In the end, the fiscal reform and the *Erfassung der Sachwerte* ended in a feeble compromise that proved a blunt weapon, if a weapon at all, in the fight against inflation. There were some adjustments to existing taxes, expecially indirect ones, but the real innovation, the panacea, was to be a compulsory loan equivalent to 1 milliard gold marks, yielding no interest for the first three years and thereafter bearing only a modest interest rate. It was the first official deviation from the sacred fiction, "mark equals mark", but in fact it was an illusion. The proceeds from the loan went "the way of all money" — in the terminology of the Inflation, "down the drain". For its "inflation-proof" character was vitiated by the fact that the government was forced to accept a clause stating that it was payable in paper marks at the rate of 70 paper marks for one gold mark. Moreover, under pressure from the interested parties, the final date for paying the loan had to be postponed. Meanwhile, the international exchange markets did not oblige by keeping the mark stable. The final result was that the actual sum collected by the Treasury amounted to only 35 to 50 million gold marks — a drop in the ocean, and quite insufficient to straighten out the monetary chaos. The revenue from normal taxation followed suit.

If the State income from taxation and compulsory loan seemed fated to be swallowed up by inflation, in some fields the government seemed positively determined to keep its revenue on a ridiculously low level. This was particularly true of railway fares and postal charges, which dropped to small fractions of their real pre-war rates. Whether it was simple inertia due to the difficulty of making more timely adjustment to the galloping depreciation of the mark, or a tender feeling for the interests of trade and commerce that wished to keep their business expenditure low, or perhaps a desire to give the hard-hit population a little pleasure by encouraging their travel mania, the public administration was unnecessarily tardy in bringing the tariffs up to date and so renounced, apparently quite deliberately, one weapon for keeping inflation within bounds.

As parliamentary and public discussions showed, in 1922 stabilisation of the mark was in the air. To be sure, at that time business, industry and agriculture were not doing too badly out of the Inflation, and the workers, even if they did not see their real wages rise to pre-war levels, at least felt that it kept them in employment.

The world at large was interested in seeing the mark stabilised as the key to the reconstruction of the world monetary system, which was on the agenda of the Genoa Conference of April 1922. Hence the request to the Bankers' Committee — the Morgan Committee as it was called — to explore the possibility of an international loan to Germany for the purpose of stabilising the mark. These efforts came to naught, as the precondition for such a loan — concessions on the reparations question — was frustrated by the inflexible attitude of the French.

All these attempts foundered on the rocks of the official doctrine that a precondition of any such operation was the restoration of the external value of the mark, and this was considered impossible without some relief from the burden of reparations payments (which, at the least, should be postponed for several years), or a foreign loan, or both.

Professor Bonn, however, did not accept this doctrine, and he put forward the alternative suggestion that the Reichsbank should make use of its gold reserves, which were still considerable, and grant the government a gold loan. This would provide the means for drawing currency out of circulation and for temporarily balancing the budget; it would also forestall any speculation against the mark.

Professor Bonn's ideas were basically in line with the verdict of the committee of experts (including Lord Keynes and Lord Brand) whose opinions on the currency question were invited by the German government. They agreed that immediate stabilisation was possible by Germany's own efforts, without an international loan and in advance of a definite reparations settlement. The report, as Viscount D'Abernon drily remarks in his memoirs, did not receive the slightest attention either from the Allies or from Germany.

The government wanted to fight inflation only on its own terms, and these were set out in a German note to the Allies on 14th November 1922. They were, in short, postponement of all obligations under the Treaty of Versailles for a period of three to four years, and a foreign loan of at least 500 million gold marks. The Allies, according to the Reichsbank's Report for 1922, unfortunately rejected these proposals, which, according to the Reichsbank, offered the only possibility of finally and definitely curing the ills of the currency. The strong French suspicion that Germany deliberately indulged in inflation in order to avoid paying its debts played a part in this rejection.

Frustrated in these efforts, the German authorities confined themselves to a number of measures designed to give some help to the ailing mark, on the one hand by penalising speculation against it, on the other by supporting it in the exchange markets. But these were merely palliatives and could not prevent the mark from depreciating further. The precious hard currency spent in the process served only to buy back the paper marks spat out so relentlessly by the printing presses.

In fact, the rejection of the German note of 14th November was the prelude to the occupation of the Ruhr in the following January, with all that that entailed in precipitating the collapse of the mark.

There were two great attacks on the Inflation in the months following the Ruhr occupation, both having some temporary success.

The first was a straightforward support action for the mark in the exchange markets; but, as the political situation arising from the Ruhr conflict demanded a defence of the currency at all costs, support was this time on a massive scale. Indeed, by buying marks and selling foreign currency, the Reichsbank succeeded in keeping the mark fairly stable — at a rate of around 20,000 to the dollar — until April 1923. But this defence really was "at all costs" and the cost proved too high. The paper money pumped out to finance the passive resistance of German labour to the French occupiers found its way into the exchange markets, and a wild speculation against the mark was set in motion. The Reichsbank had to fork out hard currency at the rate of millions of dollars every day.

"Support operations in the international exchange market", says the Reichsbank's Report for 1923, "helped only temporarily. Pessimistic views on the general situation soon led to a state of fever and panic in the exchange market. The fall of the mark was relentless and accelerated in the end in a catastrophic manner."

But the second fiscal attack in the fight against inflation did provide a short — a very short — respite. In August 1923, drastic tax increases — the "Ruhr levy" intended to cover the cost of the passive resistance — were introduced by the government.

They had, like other tax reforms in earlier periods of the inflation, a short-lived shock effect. Those who had hoarded the foreign currency previously thrown on the market by the Reichsbank were forced to sell it back in order to find the money needed to pay these taxes. The mark responded immediately and rose, but only for a few days. Another attack against the Inflation had failed, frustrated by the uninterrupted and steadily increasing volume of credit and the flow of paper marks from the printing press.

One anti-inflation weapon so familiar in our present inflationary period, the raising of the bank rate, was never really tried in earnest by the German central bank. In fact, at an earlier date it was rejected for the very reason that it would result in rising production costs and therefore rising prices and thus more inflation. The German bank rate was kept at 5 per cent until July 1922, increasing very slowly to 18 per cent in April 1923, 30 per cent in August and 90 per cent in September of that year.

Enormous as these last figures seem to be in comparison with even the very high interest rates of recent times, such rates could not, in view of the fantastic speed of depreciation of the mark, offer any compensation for losses due to the falling value of money (as the interest rates of the seventies attempt to do), or discourage the taking of credit. On the contrary, they encouraged it, and far from being a weapon in the fight against inflation, contributed to its growth.

So the mark remained sick and the government felt powerless to cure it, unless it received from abroad the wonder-drug of debt relief and loans. As it did not, the government became more or less resigned to seeing the patient die.

But, as the mark was dying, it became clear that some stable means of payment had to be found to replace it, in order to keep the wheels of economic life turning. Whatever stratagems were adopted for this purpose were not designed to rescue the mark (which was beyond redemption), nor to fight inflation, but to avert as far as possible its evil consequences.

The first moves came from the private sector. In 1921-22, businesses began to calculate and make out their invoices in gold or dollars, and wage earners followed suit by demanding that their wages be calculated in a similar way. The government obliged by issuing the basis for such calculations in the form of "indices" and "multipliers" and gradually also came to adopt similar means for its own tax demands. In August 1923, the Reichsbank itself, having been severely criticised for its preposterous policy of liberally granting credit repayable in devalued paper marks, at long last began to introduce a system of "stable" credits; borrowed money had to be repaid at a rate that took into consideration its depreciation according to an index.

But these methods proved largely unsatisfactory because the paper mark was, after all, still the actual money in which payments were made. The general need was for a real currency, a piece of paper that would not diminish in value on its way from the bank to the pay-office, from the customer to the retailer, from the retailer to the wholesaler.

In spite of warnings that, according to Gresham's Law, the bad money would drive out the good (that is to say, drive it abroad), the German authorities proceeded to create, or authorise the creation of, such good, "inflation-proof" money. It was a sort of dress rehearsal for the "miracle of the Rentenmark".

A government gold loan totalling 270 million gold marks was issued, characteristically in very small denominations, expressed in pre-war values of the dollar (for instance, 8·40 gold marks = 2 dollars, the dollar being the "round figure", in fact the primary basic sum). Unlike every other bond, this was intended to be used as a circulating means of payment, in fact as inflation-proof money. The Reich's railways also issued stable money tokens (called Oeser dollars, after the Minister of Transport) for a total of 150 million gold marks. A special decree permitted the issue of stable emergency money under certain safeguards. There were a number of similar issues in Hamburg, as Harold Fraser reported home on 27th October 1923:

> In the meantime the government scheme of issuing stabilised marks is proceeding slowly but surely. A Rentenbank has been formed and it is hoped that the Rentenmark issued by this bank on the basis of

its gold capital will appear in the first week of November. In Hamburg, however, owing to the great delay of the government, a private bank has been formed, supported by about 50 of the banks and export houses, who have each subscribed £5,000 making a total of £250,000. This bank is called the Hamburgische Bank von 1923 and has been formed primarily to open gold mark accounts for business firms. Temporarily, however, gold notes have been issued in denominations of 5, 10, and 20 marks, so that the workers in Hamburg may receive wages on a firm basis.

These notes appeared yesterday, and there are great hopes that we may receive our next week's wages in gold and not in paper marks...

It was indeed a sign of better things to come. Though the government's fight to rescue the paper mark was lost, the struggle to beat the chaos of the Inflation by giving the people a new and stable currency was beginning. It was a battle that had, in the end, to be fought and won not only in government offices, but, even more, in the minds of the people, to prevent the madness sweeping the nation from taking over absolutely.

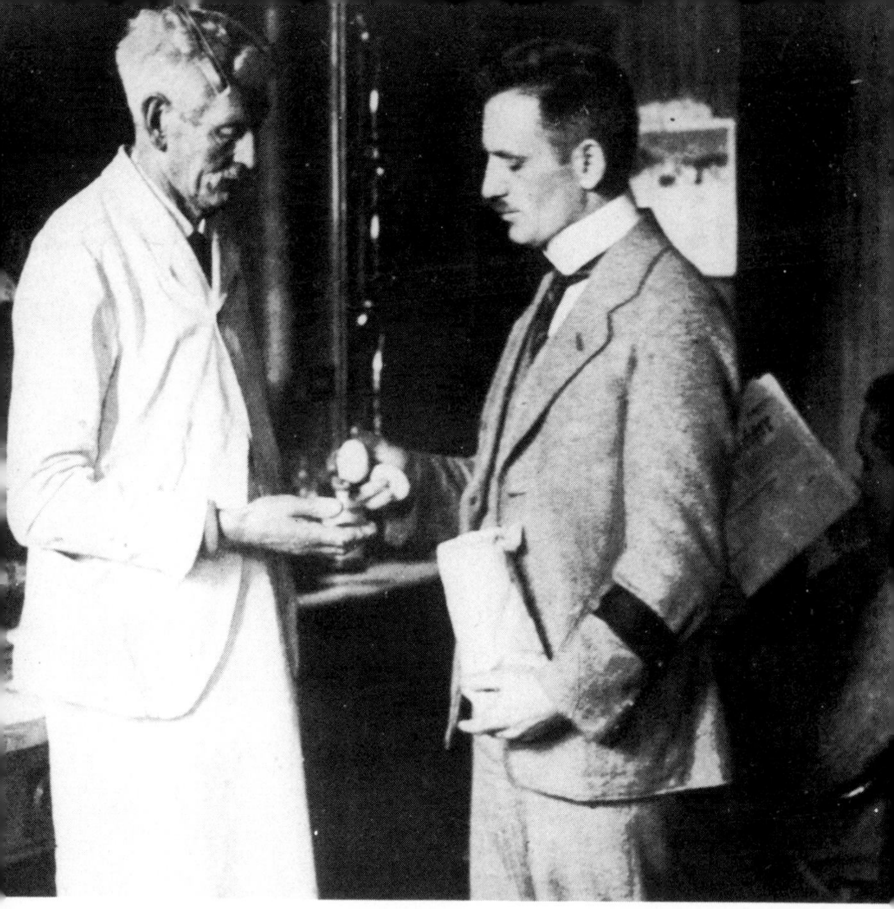

At the barber's: "Shave—two eggs; haircut—four eggs."

At the cobbler's: "Sale and repair in exchange for foodstuffs."

No. 1158 Mk. 500.000.000.000.—

Fünfhundert Milliarden Mark

in deutscher Reichswährung
vergütet die Gewerbebank Thailfingen e. G. m. u. H. in Tailfingen
dem Vorzeiger dieser Anweisung.

TAILFINGEN, den 9. November 1923.

Gewerbebank Thailfingen e. G. m. u. H.

500 Milliarden Mk.

Es wird gebeten, während der Zeit der Geldknappheit diese Anweisung in Zahlung zu nehmen.

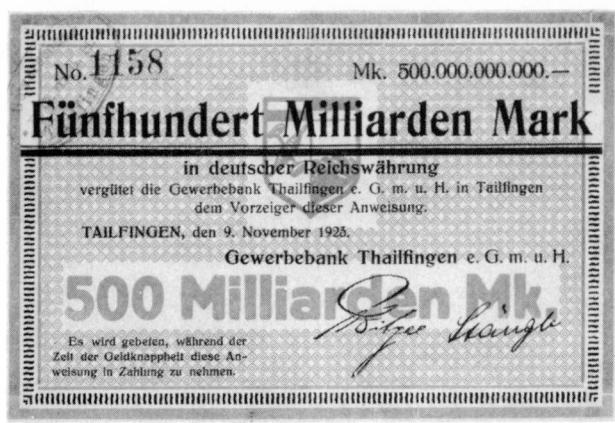

At the cinema: "Showing this afternoon: 'Judas'. Admission—two coal bricks."

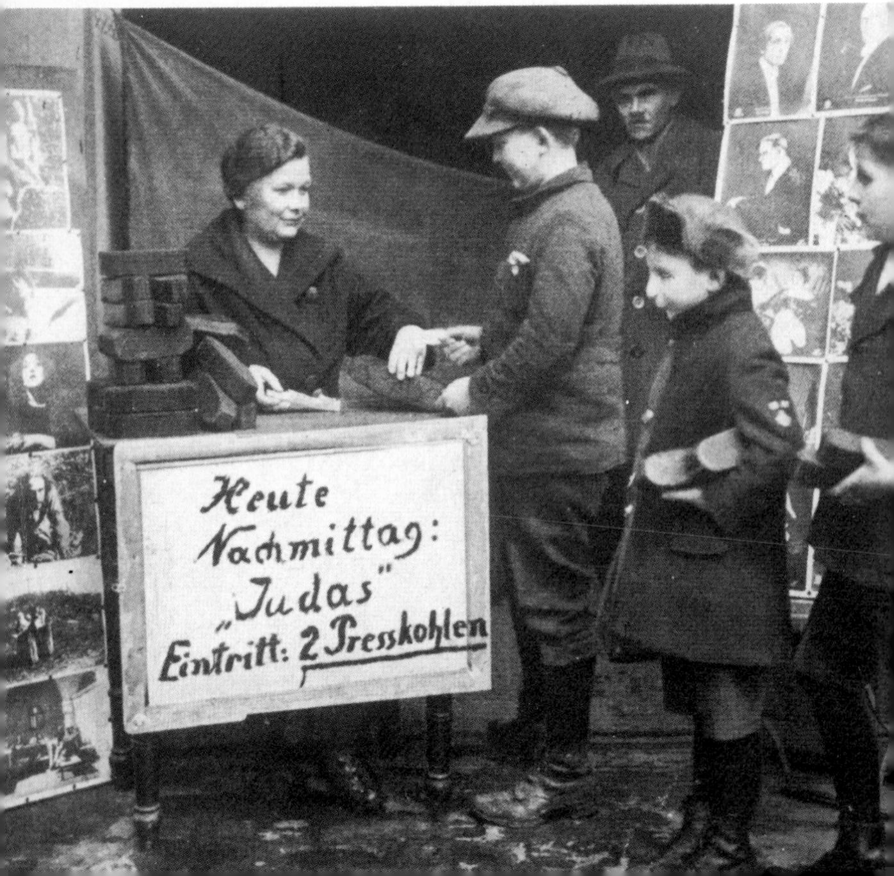

A small boy helps to tread down vast quantities of
valueless marks being prepared for pulping.

The back of a million mark note is more useful than the front!

Children use bundles of banknotes to make a kite.

Reichsbahndirektion Stuttgart.
Gutschein
Reihe 1.   Nr. 40982

Fünf Billionen Mark

dieser Gutschein wird von der Eisenbahnhauptkasse Stuttgart eingelöst,
im Wege der Verrechnung, sofort, in bar nach Behebung der gegenwärtigen
Bargeldknappheit, der Zeitpunkt der Bareinlösung wird im Staats-Anzeiger
für Württemberg und durch Anschlag auf den Bahnhöfen bekanntgegeben werden.

Stuttgart, den 9. November 1923.
Präsident

*Victims of the
Inflation forced to
offer their
valuables for sale
on the streets.*

*The new poor: many
elderly middle-class
people were kept alive
by the "people's
kitchen" organised by
charity.*

A lorry load of Hitler's stormtroopers in Munich at the time of the putsch, November 1923.

Hugo Stinnes, the legendary Inflation tycoon. (Radio Times Hulton Picture Library)

Dr Hjalmar Schacht, the man who brought
about stabilisation and launched the
Rentenmark.
(*Radio Times Hulton Picture Library*)

The Rentenmark–the new stable
currency–which only succeeded because
the public desperately wished to believe in it.

Chapter 7

The Madness of it All

Stefan Zweig, whose moving story about the Inflation, "The Invisible Collection", has already been mentioned in these pages, described in his memoirs, *Die Welt von Gestern* ("The World of Yesterday"), his horror at watching the spectacle of Berlin in the grip of the Inflation. He likened that scene, with the mushrooming of places of vulgar and coarse amusement, with its male prostitutes parading along the Kurfürstendamm, to a witches' Sabbath; the dances of homosexuals of both sexes, to orgies transcending those of decadent Rome. "Amid the general collapse of values, a kind of insanity seized precisely those middle-class circles which had hitherto been unshakeable in their order." He speaks of 16-year-old schoolgirls who would have felt insulted by the suggestion that they had still preserved their virginity.

Hans Fürstenberg in his memoirs (*Erinnerungen*) describes the nauseating display of nude shows, perverts' night clubs, and gourmets' restaurants in the city. Berlin was dancing on a volcano, leading a life of unprecedented levity without giving a thought to what the next day might bring; in spite of political upheavals, financial disarray and the misery of the poor.

In Pearl Buck's *How it Happens* . . .inflation is seen as the culminating point of the moral decay that the First World War had started.

One has to take such sweeping statements of moral indignation and condemnation — and there are many of them — with a pinch, albeit a very small pinch, of salt. To some extent they re-echo partisan propaganda and judgements that were made at the time and sound pretty hollow today. Take, for instance, Arthur Schnitzler's play *Reigen* ("Round Dance"), which reactionary agitators made the target of violent and persistent protests against its alleged immorality. In fact it was far less outspoken than the film version made in the nineteen-fifties — *La Ronde*. George Grosz, the artist, was accused of blasphemy because, as a pacifist protest, he had depicted Jesus Christ wearing a gas mask. Albert Einstein was denigrated as a destroyer of absolute values. In all these cases immorality and decadence were largely used as a stick to beat the hated republic in which such things were possible.

Altogether the great Whore of Babylon, Berlin, when seen through modern eyes, evokes in some respects nothing worse than the image of a "swinging city". To be sure, the collapse of money led to a revaluation of all values, but this also brought forth a certain creative criticism, however cynical, and a groping for new ideas and forms of expression.

There were new stirrings in the art of the cinema — witness the film *The Cabinet of Dr Caligari* (1920). The German theatre was flourishing and on its way to the world supremacy that it reached a few years later. The satirical cabaret turned the mood of despair and irreverence inherent in the Inflation period to good account, and gained the status which, only many years later, made it a model for the world at large. The names Brecht (the famous playwright) and Bauhaus (the school of architecture and design founded by Walter Gropius) are intimately associated with the period, though, at the time, they too were attacked by the upholders of the old order as symbols of decay. Even in the material sense the Inflation can claim some credit, because of its beneficial effect on the employment situation.

But these brighter spots, it must be emphasised, were few in the otherwise dark and nightmarish picture.

Indeed, the whole quality of life in Germany was warped or irreparably damaged by the ravages of inflation, and it could not have been otherwise. When one of the main pillars of social life — money — collapsed, the whole building was bound to show cracks and even more substantial damage, which was both painful and ugly to behold.

The Inflation has been called the greatest expropriation of certain classes in peacetime. Operating like a levy on some groups in favour of others, it produced a shift of wealth. Some of its beneficiaries managed to preserve their share of wealth, while others spent their new, fleeting and illusory riches as quickly as possible. For those left behind there was only poverty, with all its material, moral and political consequences.

Inflation produces more inflation. Both capital and labour swell into large uncontrollable bubbles; they are misdirected and lose their worth, with a loss of quality all round.

This shift in the ownership of wealth, the impoverishment of one group and the enrichment of another,

175

engendered by the depreciation of the currency, had a number of fundamental effects on society.

In the first place, the stake that the masses of holders of mortgages, savings bank deposits, bonds, debentures and other fixed money securities had in the country's total assets was huge, amounting to thousands of millions of pre-war marks. This sum was distributed among a multitude of individuals who thus — in the economic sense — constituted what today is called a property-owning democracy. How these personal and modest fortunes were wiped out and how the ownership of the national assets became concentrated in the fewer hands of an oligarchy has already been described. But the class that suffered was the custodian of the old-fashioned virtues, and as it disintegrated personal morality and standards of behaviour went with it.

As Otto Derkow remarks, "The Inflation was an adventure for the young ones, not for the old. For the old ones that was a breakdown of morale, ethics and everything. That was a thing abhorred and they just couldn't cope with it." For instance, the unceasing decline in the value of money discredited and made nonsense of the puritan virtue of thrift and the accumulation of wealth as the reward of hard work. Mr C.S., a currency dealer, describes how the old values were reversed for the younger generation.

It was in many ways a cheerful time for the young. When I grew up we were taught to save money and not to throw it away. It was a rather austere principle. But in the worst days of the Inflation this principle was turned upside down. We knew that to hold on to money was the worst thing we could do. So this allowed us, with a very good conscience, to spend whatever we had available. There was no question of accumulation of any capital and just this impossibility released us from the responsibility. We could disobey our parents' teaching without any feeling of guilt.

This new un-serious attitude of mind on the part of youth contrasted with yet another virtue characteristic of the traditional life of the German middle class, and which inflation swept away. Their unearned income had assured them a certain degree of freedom from material cares and a degree of leisure which had enabled them to play a distinguished rôle in the cultural and social life and progress of the nation. With the selective impoverishment of this class, culture was abandoned for the starker business of finding ways of earning a living.

This, at first sight, seems to be a healthy development. In reality it was so only to a limited degree, quite apart from the already-mentioned real loss to society resulting from the decline of that class. Just as the new super-rich had built their fortunes on speculation rather than on creative production, only too many of those now forced to earn money streamed into occupations concerned with commerce and trading, becoming dealers, agents, middlemen, hawkers, or spivs, contact men and other underlings of the big profiteers. Summarily characterising these types as parasites, a contemporary observer Franz Eulenburg, writing soon after the stabilisation, singles out the flowering of the profession of "tax consultant" (men mainly engaged in helping bigger fish to swindle the tax authorities) as a typical example of the hypertrophy of mere money manipulations. The influx from these new reservoirs of labour into the pool of manual workers was remarkably small.

In a similar way, even where the activities of the newcomers to the realm of money-making were directed towards sound and legitimate business, this affected the overall quality of life adversely. When the great Inflation profiteers, in their drive for "concentration of industry", acquired old-established firms as easy prey, such non-material values as tradition and family pride suffered, even if efficiency profited. The same happened in the case of many small and middle-sized shops and other enterprises that were fully or partly forced out of business or taken over by the more aggressive newcomers, who proliferated like weeds. The old shopkeepers and traders and merchants lost their status, and honesty and the tradition of personal service declined, to the detriment of the community.

The very manner in which the fortunes made from the Inflation were built up had a similarly detrimental effect on the quality of life. In the old days, the great fortunes of Germany (apart from the feudal and the inherited ones) had originated in some creative, productive work, such as the inventions of the Krupps in the steel industry, the Siemens in the field of electricity, and the protagonists of the great chemical industry. The new rich were not producers, or creators of industries, but mainly speculators clever enough to recognise and exploit the possibilities of the Inflation and to buy up enterprises created by others through ingenious Stock-Exchange operations, gambling on the exchange rate of the mark. Their get-rich-quick techniques became models for others as the Inflation gathered momentum and the opportunities for speculative profits increased. The figures of the *Schieber* and the *Raffke* — both slang names for profiteer, from *schieben* (to push or shift) and *raffen* (to snatch or grab) — who had made their first appearance during wartime, became more numerous. They naturally had a bad effect on the moral climate of the country, both by their behaviour and that of their acolytes, and by the bitterness and hatred they aroused among the rest of the population.

Of all the features of the Inflation, the one that perhaps made the greatest impact on the national life was the phenomenon of the "flight into *Sachwerte*", that feverish rush to exchange collapsing currency for material things.

It started with what today is called "impulse buying", but the motive for purchasing an article was not its usefulness or the pleasure it might provide, but simply the desire to possess it, to prevent someone else from getting it; hence the widespread hoarding of exotic perfumes or soaps, hairpins, telescopes, bric-à-brac and a thousand other articles of no practical use whatsoever to the owner. On a higher scale there was the acquisition of what could be termed "investments" — country houses, antiques, *objets d'art*, jewellery, luxury goods of all descriptions.

There was an even more distasteful aspect to all this. In Zweig's story, "The Invisible Collection", the narrator explains why, in his search for art treasures for sale, he visited the protagonist of the story:

> The *nouveaux riches* have suddenly discovered their taste for gothic madonnas, for incunabulas, for old prints and pictures — they would like to buy the cuff links off my sleeve, the table lamp off my desk . . . there is no resisting the onslaught of the sudden buying mania of these people . . .

So these precious things, having given pleasure to many a connoisseur now stricken with poverty, ended up in the

179

hands of a few parvenus who might just as well have collected such *Sachwerte* as waste paper or copper wire. It was a true degradation of the nation's cultural inheritance.

Worse still, these people's indiscriminate buying produced a lowering of tastes and standards of quality; if they could not get objects of the highest quality, second- or third-rate articles would do. Painters of little talent were suddenly able to sell their works — kitsch was much appreciated and enjoyed booming sales. Altogether the appreciation of old craftmanship and traditional skills diminished, and it is significant that during the Inflation the differentials between the wages for skilled and unskilled workers narrowed appreciably; the same happened with the salaries of highly qualified and less qualified public servants.

The new rich bought up the country houses and town residences that their owners could no longer afford. Scarce building resources were channelled into the construction of new luxury villas, and new and elegant suburbs grew up around Berlin. Carl Fürstenberg alluded with caustic wit to the sinister aspect of this development, which coincided with the tug-of-war about reparations. He commented, "The reconstruction of the war-ravaged north of France took place in Dahlem" — one of Berlin's fashionable and expanding suburbs.

The ostentatious display of luxury went on in full view of people who were destitute and desperate. H. G. Soameson, who lived in the fashionable Kurfürsten-damm in Berlin, remembers watching boys in their teens escorting their mistresses, who were wrapped in furs, on their customary Sunday afternoon promenades. These were the young spivs, quick-witted enough to take advantage of a situation that was beyond their elders.

The often stupid ostentation of the "haves" increased the bitterness of the "have-nots". Some of the very rich studiously avoided this ostentation. Hugo Stinnes shunned the limelight and did not make a show of his riches in the places where the big money was spent. He preferred to own the places.

In its Annual Reports for 1922 and 1923, the Reichsbank complained about the diversion of meagre resources, including foreign currency, into the excessive acquisition of *Sachwerte* and luxury goods — both durable and for consumption — which adversely affected the availability of foreign currency by also diminishing the amount of goods for export.

Quite apart from the economic damage wrought by these practices, they were also a manifestation of the spirit of selfishness and disregard for the common weal. More often than not, the flight into *Sachwerte* was prompted by greed, by the desire to obtain a material advantage at the expense of one's neighbour, and the motive to possess rather than enjoy.

This greed for possession was boundless and unashamed. Mrs Schlegel described the macabre and disgusting incident of the local parson who demanded as payment for her father's funeral service one of the last remnants of the vanished family fortune — the silver spoons. Such lack of inhibitions, quite apart from the comparatively honourable motive of desperate poverty, made the stealing of anything within reach a common practice. Willy Derkow still remembers the peak that the petty crime rate reached:

> There was not a copper pipe, not one brass armature, not a sheet of lead on the roofs that was safe. They just vanished overnight. Petrol and paraffin reached

a fantastic price on the black market. No car was safe unless someone was keeping an eye on it to prevent the petrol being siphoned out.

And in spite of rich uncles in South Africa and a respectable middle-class home, Mrs Morley remembers, "My brother was a terrible boy. He went around and screwed off metal door knobs and metal number plates from doors and went and sold them." Even railway carriages were not safe from their passengers. They were invariably stripped of their curtains and leather window-straps. This stolen property would find its way into the system of exchange and barter, which eventually took over the normal function of the shops.

Willy Derkow recalls:

> . . . You very often bought things that you did not need. But with those things in hand you could start to barter. You went round and exchanged a pair of shoes for a shirt or a pair of socks for a sack of potatoes; some cutlery or crockery, for instance, for tea or coffee or butter. And this process was repeated until you eventually ended up with the thing you actually wanted.

The Germany of the Inflation was an Eldorado for the agents, the middlemen, the spivs, who would conduct their business sometimes at street corners, sometimes in murky cafes, but mostly in the shoddy luxury of bars and night-clubs, which were springing up everywhere. These transactions did not always conform to the highest tenets of law and morality. There were illicit deals in foreign currency, in stolen or smuggled goods, sometimes in goods that did not exist at all. "We had a new word in the language," writes Hilde Homer, *"Schieber* — pushers. These men bought and sold often non-existent goods, like railway wagons of coal or minerals." A considerable part of the activities of these agents was the finding of customers for the new poor forced to part with their valuables in order to keep alive. Mrs Ehrhardt recalls one of the meaner tricks current at the time:

> The racketeer used to "test" ornaments or jewellery offered to him for sale. He would scrape off a little gold, pronounce the object to be of little value and — if the owner was desperate — thus acquire it from him for a small sum. Even if he didn't actually buy whatever it was, as time went on he acquired a useful amount of gold scrapings!

The logical need to spend money quickly and the hectic life of insecurity and fear to which people were condemned combined in creating tensions. The result was to seek an outlet for, so to speak, both the money and the tensions. "People shook with hysteria when the new dollar rate was published, and the first row with a girl friend made them blow their brains out", wrote Carl Zuckmayer in his memoirs, describing the Berlin scene. Gambling was widespread and many gambling dens attracted customers in search of excitement and eager to get rid of their money. Prostitutes of both sexes were in demand and they flourished; not stark poverty alone, but also the temptation to make easy money (all the better when it was a dollar note) was an effective recruiting agent for the oldest profession. Drug-taking became fashionable and a vast army of peddlers and pushers supplied the addicts and the beginners, who, out of a sense of frustration or the desire to discover a new and expensive thrill, were to become addicts in their turn. The word "cocaine" was a symbol of the age and entered the repertoire of the literary cabarets. There were bars, night-clubs, dance-halls in abundance, to suit every fancy.

How little the people cared whether they got any real value for their money (if that money still had any value at all) was shown by the emergence of what was called the *Kellerromantik* (cellar romanticism): makeshift drinking-dens in disused cellars where bottled beer was dispensed at extortionate prices in an often completely bogus atmosphere of vice, crime and general immorality; and where customers were happy to empty their pockets in order to enjoy these wholly artificial excitements.

But for most people, life during these inflation years was a matter of animal, sordid, grinding poverty; the real lack of means to buy goods in the same way as before the Inflation, or even to buy the sheer necessities of life in sufficient quantities.

A telling, if rather homely, example of this deterioration was the condition of salaried employees. These people, though their incomes covered the bare necessities of life, were unable to buy clothing, household goods and similar semi-durable goods. Mrs Ehrhardt's mother made dresses for her out of a red woollen table cloth, even out of mattress covers; and she had "underwear made from the white section of an old and out-of-date flag!"

Now, bearing in mind that a decent wardrobe and a well-filled linen cupboard were, for that class, a part of pride and self-esteem, there is significance in the remark of a financial journalist in 1923 that "an analytical inventory of the linen owned by those classes" would be the best statistical evidence of their diminished standard of living and morale.

As the mark plunged towards the abyss, food virtually disappeared from the shops. Farmers simply would not sell for paper money. Any supplies that did get through had to run the gauntlet of desperate people. A Salvation Army worker noted, "There is a great scarcity of potatoes at present because of the danger of transport. They can't be carted in the daytime or they would be stolen. They are brought in at night from the country, covered up."

In a statement made in February 1923, the Head of the Public Health Department listed the ills that resulted from these conditions: mortality in general was rising as a consequence of diseases provoked by malnutrition; the incidence of stomach disorders and of scurvy was growing; typhoid and skin diseases had become more frequent because of a lack of hygiene in the handling of food; pneumonia and rheumatic complaints increased among those too poor to buy warm clothing and fuel. Children in particular suffered, infant mortality increased and so did rickets and tuberculosis. Schoolchildren were underweight.

There were occasions when, in Berlin, thousands of gallons of milk remained unsold because people could not afford to buy. Indeed, as time went on it was not even available to those who could. Mrs Kaufmann's harrowing experience when, as a young mother, she went to stay with her parents-in-law in Berlin, bears witness to the coarsening effect the stress of life had on people's natures:

> You couldn't get any milk unless you had a certificate that you had a baby. As a visitor to the city, I went to the nearest dairy to register for milk. The

> woman behind the counter was very unpleasant and
> said quite roughly, "We haven't any milk for you."
> "But", I said, "I have a small baby and I'm entitled
> to it," and she said, "Why do you bring babies into
> the world — drown it!"

The consumption of beef dropped by 50 per cent as
compared with 1913; that of pork even more; whilst the
consumption of horse meat (though this represented only
a very small proportion of meat consumption) did not
show any change. Dr Herbert Lawton has a ghoulish
story to tell, arising from the difficulties of procuring
meat:

> I was a student at Friedrich Wilhelm University in
> Breslau and my brother and I were in lodgings in
> Sadowa Street near the main railway station. Meat
> was in short supply and so expensive hardly anyone
> could afford to buy it. But still our landlady kept us
> generously supplied. When we asked her how she
> did it, she said she travelled to Münsterberg every
> Thursday where she could buy as much as she
> wanted and not too expensively. Imagine our shock
> when we learned later that Münsterberg was the
> centre from which the mass-murderer Denke
> conducted his operations!

One detail, however small, is worth mentioning, if only
as a sign of the times: what was in Germany an almost
legendary symbol of famine — the eating of dogs — was
practised. 1,090 dogs were slaughtered for human
consumption in the third quarter of 1921; 3,678 in the
third quarter of 1922; 6,430 in the corresponding quarter
of 1923.

There were not sufficient funds for medical care, the equipment and provisioning of hospitals, the supply of drugs and medicines. Even the dead were not spared the humiliations of poverty. As the cost of burials rocketed, official permission was given for the use of cheap coffins — made of paper.

Welfare institutions, whose income was mainly derived from investment of the kind that was wiped out by inflation, were tragically restricted in their functions. It is characteristic that, in Berlin alone, the total assets of such bodies, which originally amounted to some 56 million gold marks were reduced by the Inflation to little more than 1 million. But the Salvation Army carried on. They used to go visiting in their neighbourhoods to see who needed help.

> We'd find people in their beds, too weak to get up and too proud to beg. Our doctor told us about two elderly sisters, unmarried, whose parents had left them well provided for. The money had evaporated and they were starving. We sent them a dinner every day which kept them alive, but many others starved to death.

Just as the standards of well-being declined, so did those of intellectual life. The degradation of that section of the middle class that had traditionally provided recruits for the world of science, learning and cultural progress in general led to a drying up of that source; and the old link between *Besitz und Bildung* — between affluence, in the sense of financial independence, and culture — snapped. Remaining energies were devoted to the pursuit of money-making rather than of cultural values. To this was added the fact that outside funds for the support of learning and research — legacies, foundations, bequests — were curtailed by inflation.

Also as a result of the Inflation, there were no longer adequate funds available for the purchase of the essential tools for scientific research. Take, for instance, the case of microscopes. The development and manufacture of these instruments had been one of the glories of the German optical industry, as the names of Zeiss and Leitz testify, and the achievements of these companies had in turn assured to German natural science the leading rôle in such branches of medicine as bacteriology. The price of a high quality microscope, some 1,000 gold marks before the war, had risen by 1923 to an astronomical amount of paper marks, and the allocations from public funds were simply insufficient for such purchases. In fact, whatever the manufacturers of such goods were able to produce was promptly snapped up by foreign buyers able, on the strength of their own currencies, to buy them at bargain prices for the benefit of the scientists of their own countries. But their gain was naturally the loss of their German colleagues, whose work had to suffer.

The price of books and learned publications of all kinds rose in keeping with that of other material goods and put them out of the reach of the individual scholar; worse still, even the public institutions, libraries, universities and so on were unable to buy them, since the allocation of funds was lagging way behind the rate of inflation.

On the other hand, the intellectual workers, the scholars who wrote those highly priced books, were badly underpaid. One member of the German Reichstag, Dr Schuster, who happened to be the editor of a learned journal, revealed that his remuneration by the end of 1922 had never risen above the pre-war level. The salaried members of the faculties of the universities and other institutions of learning, the eminent German professors, were in the position of high-ranking civil servants and as such were severely affected by the drop in their real incomes caused by the Inflation. Their peace of mind, and with it their capacity for creative work, diminished as a result of psychological stress and material deprivation. Some were compelled to sell their valuables and the libraries essential for their work just to keep themselves and their families alive.

Georg Schreiber, writing while the Inflation was still in progress, made the sombre observation, "Years of paper currency mean no more and no less than the decline of learning and, if the sickness of the currency lasts a long time, the eventual death of learning and science."

Many of these brain workers had to resort to manual work in order to feed their families — to the detriment, of course, of their real vocation.

Sheer poverty was understandably the main cause of the growth of prostitution and criminal activity, for which the moral decline of the Inflation provided the fertile soil. As far as crime is concerned, the available statistics speak for themselves. The total number of convictions rose from 562,000 in 1913 to 826,000 in 1923, but more significant for an explanation of the typical criminal mentality of the Inflation is the fact that the number of thefts, the taking of *Sachwerte*, rose in that same period from 115,000 to 365,000. In the case of young men the rate of increase was much higher than the average — even in this field the older generation proved less adaptable to the conditions of inflation!

With devaluation of the currency had come devaluation

of most of the old virtues: the respect for law and order, for morality, for one's fellow men, the simple and contemplative life, thrift, even good taste and the appreciation of the truly good things of life. But one virtue, to all intents and purposes, seemed not only to have survived but also to have become more universal: industriousness. Indeed, with the exception of the last few catastrophic months of the Inflation and a few intermittent setbacks, German industry and its work force were very active, and the rest of the population were busy in offices and shops (and, of course, in agriculture) or frantically plying all sorts of trades in order to turn an honest — or not so honest — penny.

"Es wird viel gearbeitet" — a lot of work is being done, a contemporary observer remarked. Alas, much of this work was partly or even totally unproductive, or the product was not of the right kind. The Inflation had also inflated work, diluted it, and diminished its quality and usefulness.

This was shown first of all in the physical activity of the individual.

The lowering of the standards of nutrition meant that the worker's intake of calories was insufficient to keep his energies up to full requirements. As Churchill remarked at one phase of the Second World War, "A miner cannot work all out if he is fed on cabbage sandwiches." At that time the Americans obliged by sending Spam; but during the Inflation there was no Spam for German workers.

Then there were the constant tensions and worries caused by the vagaries of the Inflation, the eternal struggle to adapt wages to rising prices, the unceasing preoccupation with the dollar rate, the often futile rush to convert wages into the necessities of life — all this adversely influenced the will to work, the intensity of work, its quality and productivity. Much loss was also caused through the careless handling of machines and materials when the worker's strength and concentration were reduced.

Any decline in the output of the productive worker, the worker who really makes things, meant that overall productivity was further diminished by the disproportionate addition, due to the inflationary conditions, of more and more "non-productive" employees. Reduced to its simplest terms, the problem was that an entry into a ledger which in normal times might have run, on average, to three or four digits, at the height of the Inflation might easily have been ten or twelve. The Reichsbank's Balance Sheet for 1923 culminates in a 24-digit figure. Accountancy in these circumstances became maddening. Firms had to set up special offices for wages accounting and foreign currency accounting.

The complications of coping with the unceasing changes in the dollar rate and the "multiplier", and the instantaneous application of these changes to wages, salaries, sales and purchases, required the attention of armies of office staff. The story is told of a huge printing plant where the management just transferred the compositors and linotype operators from their machines and work benches into the offices to get on with the paper-work, for which these people were anything but qualified. The big industrial firm of Siemens-Schuckert worked out that whereas in 1913 there were 0·537 office employees for every worker on the production line, the figure had risen in 1923 to 0·766. In other words, with all the calculating and form-filling so characteristic of the Inflation, three people were needed to do the paper-work normally handled by two.

Typical was the influx of employees into the banking industry, that branch of the economy above all devoted to the unproductive task of handling the masses of inflation-generated money, and the shuffling around of existing assets without in any way increasing them. The total number of bank employees almost quadrupled between 1914 and 1923, from about 100,000 to 375,000; the personnel of the Reichsbank in 1923 alone increased from 13,316 to 22,909. What was worse, the need for additional staff sprang from the extra work of counting and distributing banknotes. For this task, men and women without skill and, consequently, with limited efficiency had to be used, almost exclusively. Precious material and labour were diverted into the erection of new buildings to accommodate, as the joke went, noughts — the noughts that made the ledgers grow and created the armies of clerks whose "real value" was zero.

Moreover, in offices all over Germany the routine work of the staff suffered from their preoccupation with their own financial interests. We have already seen how bank clerks were deeply involved in Stock-Exchange speculations; in general, employees were desperately preoccupied with buying, selling and bartering all sorts of goods, not missing opportunities for getting some extra food, in all places of work. It was as though people nowadays were to spend their working time filling in football pools, not just for a short period once a week, but for hours every day.

Banking and commerce of every description attracted labour at the expense of true production. As one of Germany's leading bankers, Max Warburg, remarked, "A nation that makes the wrong use of its labour force, conducts its economy in the wrong way."

There was no lack of candidates for that kind of purely

commercial job. Eulenburg speaks of the "much-too-many" who, having seen their circumstances reduced by the Inflation, competed for a share in the more profitable opportunities it afforded.

There were the freelance dealers, and such familiar types as spivs, agents, drug peddlers, middlemen, and small-scale speculators, who led a twilight hand-to-mouth existence. But equally important was the fact that the inflated volume of existing businesses had led to their absorbing large numbers of underlings and that new businesses, one-man enterprises and small partnerships set up by people seeking a new source of income proliferated.

Again, banking offers the most telling example of this development. In 1914 the number of newly-opened banks was 42; in 1923 the number was more than 400. The business of the big German banks grew enormously, as evidenced by the fact that the number of current accounts — largely engendered by the huge volume of Stock-Exchange transactions — was in 1923 five times as many as in 1913. Some of the newcomers to banking were solid enterprises that operated on traditional lines, or acted in the merger and takeover deals of the great tycoons. The great majority however, were mushroom growths, viable only in the hectic climate of the Inflation; indeed, with the stabilisation of the currency most of them went out of business. Many of them were simply money-changers. In the border areas of the country especially, where large amounts of foreign notes flowed across the frontiers — legitimately or not — one-man or two-men businesses of this type were hurriedly set up. For instance, an enterprising doctor whose practice had vanished would find a dismissed bank clerk and open, under some high-sounding name, a money-changing business in a nearby shop.

The Great Inflation

This growth was by no means confined to the banking world. Altogether the number of limited companies of all kinds trebled between 1913 and 1923.

As for one-man businesses and partnerships, an average of 30,000 firms were established in each of the Inflation years (as against 10,000 in 1913). In 1923 the number of new registrations jumped to around 4,600 *per month*. A large proportion of these were retail shops, many of which were engaged in selling second-hand goods. Their stock-in-trade consisted of the possessions that the new poor were forced to sell in order to eat. One realises how inflated and overmanned, how remote from the solid business tradition of the old days, these beehive activities were, if one bears in mind that, owing to the widespread scarcity of new goods, total turnover was less than in pre-war days. It was simply the number of useless hands through which the goods passed that had multiplied.

The scarcity of consumer goods was reflected in the depressed purchasing power and standard of living of the consuming public, and production of such goods consequently declined. On the other hand, there was an increase in the production of the means of production — new plant, machinery, industrial equipment of all kinds.

The capacity of dockyards, for instance, was doubled as ships of all flags converged on Germany for their repairs. The dockyards, benefiting from the depressed exchange rate of the mark, were able to undercut their foreign competitors.

On the face of it this investment boom would seem a healthy development, a solid foundation for general prosperity. In reality it was not quite so, as regards either the motives behind it or the results it had.

Originally, large investments in capital goods stemmed

194

from the unobjectionable intention to make good the ravages of the war and to restore the heavily impaired productive capacity of the country. But, later, and increasingly as time went on, investment in capital and non-consumer goods was but part of the general pattern of behaviour: the flight into *Sachwerte,* the need to convert money into "tangible goods". Thus the "winners" — like the little man who would buy anything rather than hold on to banknotes — were in a hurry to purchase, often indiscriminately, equipment, machinery, buildings — indeed, whatever was available — as *Sachwerte,* regardless of actual need. Farmers did the same and indulged in what was called a flight from the mark to the machine, with the result that the collection of machinery in the hands of farmers far exceeded their real needs. And whilst the machine manufacturers made machines and the builders built factories and commercial premises, the ordinary people went without adequate housing, clothing and food. It was a sad and tragic situation.

Additional means of production did not lead to greater productivity and efficiency. To put it in a nutshell: *capacity* for production increased compared to 1913, but *actual production* declined. One reason for this was, as has already been mentioned, that the expansion of capital investment was made for expansion's sake, often to conceal high profits and save them from the tax collector, rather than for the sake of productivity and efficiency. Often firms just bought more machines, not better ones. For much of the Inflation period real wages were low, so there was no pressure from the wages side to introduce labour-saving techniques and machinery.

Another reason was that the monetary chaos and the relentless and rapid fluctuation of production costs and prices made it difficult for the entrepreneur to calculate his real costs; nor could he estimate the depreciation of plant or his real profit and thus plan and organise production accordingly. As long as paper profits looked good, there was little incentive to seek for possible economies through rationalisation and increased efficiency.

Moreover, the quality of management deteriorated. Many enterprises had passed into the control of speculators, experts in manipulating stocks, shares and money rather than in running a factory. And even skilled managers were corrupted by the ease of making a speculative profit.

Finally, the general boom created by the conditions of the Inflation led to the prosperity of not only the best, the most efficient, the most valuable individuals for the processes of the economy, but also those who would not have passed the test in more normal conditions. Hence the virtual disappearance of bankruptcies — that process of weeding out the unfit by means of natural selection.

But perhaps the most terrifying effect of the inflation on the national life was the outbreak of a sort of collective insanity. That is the image that dominates the memories of eye-witnesses of the great German Inflation and the tales related by its chroniclers. Such terms as "witches' Sabbath", "an age of Bedlam of unprecedented dimensions", "a kind of lunacy gripping the people" form the *Leitmotiv* of the story and give an idea of the state of mind of a nation. They are based on impressions and personal feelings rather than on hard clinical facts, but are nevertheless true.

Even as a young boy, Leopold Ullstein was conscious of the almost manic atmosphere in which he was growing up:

People just didn't understand what was happening. All the economic theory they had been taught didn't provide for the phenomenon. There was a feeling of utter dependence on anonymous powers — almost as a primitive people believed in magic — that *somebody* must be in the know, and that this small group of "somebodies" must be a conspiracy. The sheer irrationality of the thing conveyed the feeling that people were under a spell.

As for actual medical or psychiatric diagnosis, we have to accept the word of the experts that nervous disorders — and the suicide rate — increased as a result of anxiety about the dreadful conditions caused by the Inflation, that "the psychological impoverishment of the middle classes precipitated emotional insecurities".

There was moral insanity, a diminishing ability to distinguish between right and wrong, as witnessed by the readiness of hitherto perfectly decent people to steal, forge and deceive in order to get hold of some *Sachwerte*; the disregard of the currency laws in order to obtain precious foreign exchange; the callous and almost paranoiac violation of the rights of one's fellow men in order to grab some food.

But the most direct and disruptive impact of the Inflation on men's minds was the effect of the astronomical sums of money, the dance of the millions, which pervaded the economic life of the nation and the everyday life of the individual.

Money lost its substance. The discrepancy between its appearance and real value could not but produce bewilderment and chaos in minds that had to cope with the Herculean task of juggling with these enormous, yet deceptive figures. Confusion was made worse by the fact

197

that what little meaning the figures still had was changing from hour to hour.

People had (to paraphrase Fallada) calculated, multiplied with multipliers, divided by divisors until they went out of their minds. The publication of the dollar rate twice daily set the human calculating machines spinning to figure out what wages they would receive and what they would be able to buy with them. It made them shake with hysteria.

At an early stage of the Inflation the result was a sort of megalomania: many fancied themselves real millionaires when they had a few of those large-denomination notes in their pockets, unable to understand that their illusory fortune would not even keep them in food for a couple of weeks.

Even the Reichsbank itself became infected with the public mania. Towards the end of the Inflation, when it had become clear to all that the mark was absolutely worthless, there was the grotesque spectacle of the bank recording, with a sort of lunatic solemnity, the sum of 79 pfennigs in a balance sheet that went into thousands of trillions of marks. The cost of the printing ink used for the purpose was many times the value of the pfennigs themselves.

In other financial circles they were more pragmatic in their operations. Mr C.S. describes the attitude of the foreign exchange dealers:

> When it came to those enormous denominations, we in the foreign exchange market no longer bothered to do much arithmetic. One would come to the office in the morning: well, what is the pound sterling today? (It might be one of those days when you felt sterling might rise because Poincaré had made an

unpleasant speech, for instance.) 5 million marks?
All right, buy a thousand pounds' worth. But you no
longer did any figuring. You figured only so long as
every per cent meant something, but when it came to
fluctuations of ten per cent between ten and eleven
o'clock in the morning you no longer bothered.

Befuddled by these figures, otherwise intelligent
people were just incapable of acting normally. W.G.
remembers,

> For the celebration of my brother's wedding, which
> I've mentioned in another context, it was considered
> absolutely essential for the dignity of the family that
> I should be "properly" dressed; but the resources of
> my depleted wardrobe were insufficient for the
> purpose. So I had to buy a new suit, a dinner-jacket
> and trousers, as tradition required. My mother sold
> her diamond ring — behind my father's back, for
> this unprecedented event would have been
> incompatible with the pride of a man who still
> considered himself well off — and gave me the
> proceeds: one 10 million mark note.
>
> With this precious note I proudly went to one of
> the city shops. I bought a suit, costing 8 million
> marks and tendered my note. The suit was wrapped
> up and handed to me, but I was so completely
> confused by the enormous figures involved, and
> altogether by the magnitude of the transaction, that
> it did not occur to me to pick up my change of
> 2 million marks.
>
> I walked out of the shop in a sort of trance,
> clutching my fabulous *Sachwert* under my arm —
> this was reality; the money, on that day still worth

something, was not. Only a few days later did I
remember that I ought to have a decent pair of shoes
to go with the suit, and that my mother's gift should
have bought that too. Only then did I remember the
change, and returned to the shop to claim it;
naturally I had no proof whatsoever to support my
unlikely tale; the manager just shrugged his
shoulders, pointing out to me that with the further
fall in the mark, those 2 millions were hardly worth
bothering about. So that was the end of it — the
2 millions change, after all, had only been a chimera.

Herbert Hochfeld also testifies to the degeneration of
a couple of million marks into mere small change. He
still has the letter that his mother wrote to tell him that
the cheque that came regularly from relatives in England
had gone astray. She had to send a telegram to them
saying whether it had arrived or not. The single word
"no" she told her son, cost 2,446,000 marks.

How the borderline between reality and appearance,
indeed between madness and normality, was blurred is
illustrated by a story that W.G.'s brother used to tell
about his work at the University psychiatric clinic at
Munich:

Whenever a new patient was brought in, the doctors
started their investigation with a simple test to find
out whether the patient was an obvious mental case
or whether, at least on the face of it, he was normal.
They would ask him a few elementary questions
such as: how old are you, how many children have
you got, what is the height of the Zugspitze? And the
answers could easily be, "I'm 25 million years old,
have 1,000 or 15,000 children, etc."

The figures varied very much, one suspects, with the changing dollar rate; but the problem remained. Was the patient simply confused by the large figures that dominated his daily life, was it a slip of the tongue, was he obsessed by these figures, or was he just stark, raving mad? A person's attitude towards daily life during the Inflation was no longer a yardstick for judging the state of his mind. People, indeed, found it difficult to assess the meaning of numbers not related to money.

For instance, there took place at that time an all-German rally of athletes in Munich, and the influx of visitors into the town was enormous by any standards. Fantastic tales were circulating about the exploits of these people. One of them was that they stole no fewer than 6,000 beer steins from one of Munich's famous beer cellars; another was that thousands of people queued up every day to climb the Zugspitze massif. If the facts were true, then this sort of behaviour reflected only the lawlessness and recklessness which were a by-product of the times; but it is more likely that these stories were not true. Yet they were readily believed — what, after all, was the meaning of the number "6,000"?

The Inflation even blurred many leading policy makers' clarity of vision and ability to comprehend the situation. They were mesmerised by the idea that nothing could be done about the Inflation, obsessed by the self-imposed duty to provide the economy with all the finance it demanded. The pride of the Reichsbank President in his institute's ability to push more and more paper money into circulation, and the applause it earned, were a manifestation beyond the merely grotesque.

But, though the heavy responsibilities of these people must certainly have strained their nerves to the utmost, were they pathological cases?

The Great Inflation

In August 1923, the British Ambassador, Viscount D'Abernon, recorded in his diary that he despaired of Germany's ever being able to recover from the ravages of the Inflation "unless power is taken away from the lunatics at present in charge". The lunatics were clearly personified in the figure of Dr Havenstein. He died on 20th November 1923.

The lunatics were then no longer in charge. The madness of it all stopped: the Rentenmark had arrived.

Chapter 8

The Miracle
of the Rentenmark

By the beginning of November 1923 Germany's situation was desperate. In the words of the Minister of Finance, Hans Luther, "a dissolution of the social order was expected almost from hour to hour".

The Germans were facing economic chaos, political chaos, social disintegration and the threat of famine; they were drowning in the flood of paper money. The year had brought a bumper harvest but people were in acute danger of starving; though their granaries were full to bursting point, farmers were refusing to sell their corn for worthless marks.

By the end of the year the country had a sound currency; people had in their pockets money that would buy them what they wanted, when they needed it; the finances of the Reich had begun to look healthier, and the political storms had calmed down; instead of the quicksands of the Inflation, the people felt they had firm ground under their feet. There was hope for better times to come.

It was a miraculous change, and, indeed, the event

203

that had brought it about has become a legend under the name of the "miracle of the Rentenmark". It happened, to all intents and purposes, on 16th November 1923.

The miracle was produced by a combination of financial tricks, make-believe and, above all, faith. "The miracle", in the words of Goethe's *Faust*, "is the favourite child of faith."

The essential prerequisite for successfully putting an end to the Inflation was that the will to do so should be universal, embracing even those who earlier, for reasons of their own — selfish or otherwise — had seen inflation as desirable or inevitable. Some of them, incidentally, had later to be forcibly reminded not to change their minds again.

The moment of truth came in the autumn of 1923.

In the summer of that year the mark, to all intents and purposes, was dead. Economic activity, or what was left of it in that period of rapidly growing stagnation, was kept going by payments calculated, no longer in paper marks, but in gold or dollars. At the same time "stable money" — consisting mainly of the small denominations of the Reich's gold loan, the Oeser dollar, the money issued by the Hamburgische Bank of 1923 and other types of authorised stable emergency money—had tested the reaction of the public to that kind of new currency.

The result was favourable in so far as it proved that people, who so profoundly mistrusted the old marks, were eagerly putting their full confidence in the soundness of, as it was said, any piece of paper on which was printed "stable or constant value", accepting it, even hoarding it, as though it were pure gold. In fact the backing of these issues, which circulated in relatively modest quantities, was a form of words rather than a reality. But this was a successful trial run for the future

Rentenmark.

Other preparatory steps consisted in measures to alleviate the financial burden of the Reich. The most drastic came on 26th September: the passive resistance to the French occupation of the Ruhr, which had been the cause of enormous expense covered only by the printing of more money, was called off. No further loans for the purpose were forthcoming after 15th October.

This was followed by acts designed to relieve temporarily the Reich's obligations to pay reparations directly. Whether or not this really meant what Professor Elster describes as "the Reich granting to itself that moratorium which had been refused by the Allies in the past", technically, at any rate, the reparations burden was taken out of the budget and transferred on to German industry by way of the so-called Micum contracts. These were agreements between German industrialists and the Micum, the "Mission Interalliée de Contrôle des Usines et des Mines", by which a wide circle of German industrialists mainly from the Ruhr undertook to make certain payments and deliveries of a variety of goods as reparations. It was a way of paying reparations without directly involving the finances of the Reich, thus facilitating the stabilisation of the currency.

A significant point about these Micum negotiatons was that the leading light on the German side was Hugo Stinnes. It meant that those who, only recently, had been beneficiaries of the Inflation and had favoured inflation as proof of Germany's inability to pay reparations (and had therefore opposed the policy of fulfilment), now saw the light and realised that everything possible had to be done to stop inflation. The prerequisite for success in the struggle against inflation — the united front — was thus established.

This also was borne out by another fact, not devoid of irony.

Karl Helfferich, who ever since the war had been the foremost supporter of inflationary policies, an ardent opponent of fiscal and political measures that might have avoided the worst aspects of inflation, and a vicious personal enemy of those who favoured those measures, entered the arena as the champion of stabilisation.

In August 1923 he submitted a plan, in fact an elaborate draft bill, for the introduction of a new currency.

He painted a sombre — and true — picture of the situation and warned that the collapse of the mark threatened the nation with utter catastrophe. It was he who said that a large proportion of the German people were in danger of starving to death whilst the granaries were full, unless within weeks the old currency was replaced by "something new"; and he then went on to explain what, in his opinion, that "something new" should be.

This cry of alarm set the ball rolling. Helfferich has the merit not only of having taken the initiative, but also of having put forward the basic ideas that, although with many modifications, led to the Rentenmark and the stabilisation of the German economy.

Helfferich's ideas were based on the truism that money will retain its value only when the public is willing to accept it with the conviction that it can be exchanged at any time for the amount of goods or services promised by its face value. That confidence had completely vanished with regard to the paper mark; disgorged in limitless quantities by the Reichsbank, an institution itself held in contempt, it was money not worth the paper it was printed on, representing nothing and completely unacceptable.

So Helfferich envisaged a new type of money, different in both name and origin from the old one, backed by something tangible in the eyes of the recipient.

He therefore suggested the "rye mark", based on and backed by the value of that cereal, and issued by a new body — a currency bank established by the main exponents of the German economy, agriculture, industry and commerce.

His very detailed and elaborate plan was criticised (rye, it was said, was unsuitable as a yardstick of value because of the widely fluctuating price) and discussed. There were counter-proposals, and ultimately there emerged the Rentenmark plan, which incorporated many elements of Helfferich's original idea. Its legal basis was an Enabling Act of 13th October and the Decree of 15th October concerning the establishment of the Deutsche Rentenbank, which had been prepared under the auspices of Dr Hans Luther, Finance Minister since 6th October.

To put it briefly and simply: the Rentenbank was a corporate body, separate from the State, founded by the representatives of agriculture, industry and commerce. It had a capital of 3,200 million Rentenmarks (equal to that many gold marks), consisting of a charge of half the amount on the agricultural and forest land of the country, and half on its commercial and industrial enterprises.

On the strength of these charges the Rentenbank issued bonds for 500 gold marks each (one gold mark being the value of one 2,790th of a kilo of gold). These were the backing for the actual Rentenmark notes, which were issued in denominations of from one to 1,000 Rentenmarks. The bank was authorised to grant credits

207

to a total amount of 2,400 million Rentenmarks, half of this for the Reich, half for the private economy. The Rentenmark notes could be exchanged for the bonds for 500 gold marks — this was the stability factor.

Besides the issue of notes, the creation of new credit was the essential function of the new bank. The means of the Reich were exhausted; indeed, it was a condition of the credit granted to the Reich that it should use 300 million of it to buy back the treasury bonds in exchange for which it had received credits from the Reichsbank.

Thereafter the Reichsbank was not allowed to discount · any further Treasury bills for the Reich, which meant that the corresponding issue of paper marks also ceased.

The purpose of channelling the Rentenmark into the hands of the Reich was, on the one hand, to help the Reich overcome its financial difficulties — at least until such time as the measures aimed at balancing the budget by increasing tax revenues and restricting expenditure, both initiated at the same time, should bear fruit — and, on the other hand, that the chaotic conditions of the private economy should be remedied by the new monetary basis.

The private economy, which had lost most of its liquid capital either directly through the depreciation of money or by spending it on *Sachwerte,* and had therefore reached an impasse, was in dire need of cash to revive it.

These aims were ultimately crowned by success, but not without moments of crisis which threatened to frustrate the whole scheme.

As the day appointed for the issue of the Rentenmark, 16th November, approached, gigantic amounts of paper marks were in circulation. They were — and remained — the official legal currency of the Reich. The government had decided that, coinciding with the issue of the new

Rentenmark, this old money should be brought into a fixed relationship with the new one, a relationship that should be acceptable the world over. The question arose, at what rate should the old money be stabilised?

A vital part in the stabilisation of the currency was played by a banker, Dr Hjalmar Schacht, who on 12th November was appointed Reich's Currency Commissar and later President of the Reichsbank. Schacht accomplished his task with astuteness, skill and ruthlessness, and his success has earned him the title of a "financial wizard". He became almost a legendary figure, whose fame (or notoriety) endured for almost half a century, surviving the Nazi period; and he was forever giving new proof of his talents.

Schacht had been a member of the Democratic Party, and after stabilisation his name and achievement were exploited for propaganda purposes, one of the propaganda slogans then in vogue being.

> *Wer hat die Rentenmark erdacht?*
> *Der Demokrat, der Doktor Schacht,*

(Who invented the Rentenmark? Dr Schacht the Democrat).

That he was not so convinced a democrat as was assumed was demonstrated by his later associations with the arch-nationalist and reactionary circles. Nor was he the inventor of the Rentenmark — that was Finance. Minister Luther. But as the "miracle of the Rentenmark" relied so much on psychological elements, the symbolic figure of a magician waving his wand was a great contribution to its success.

Schacht was more than a magician: he was supremely clever. If the creation of the Rentenmark has been compared to constructing a roof before the house was built, Schacht surely had the merit of providing much of the building on which the roof was to rest securely.

On 12th November Schacht was confronted by a grotesque situation. The dollar was quoted on the Berlin Exchange at 630 milliard marks. In New York and Cologne (in occupied territory and therefore outside the jurisdiction of the Reich) the dollar was quoted at even more paper marks.

On that day the paper marks in circulation amounted to about 60 trillions' worth — calculated by the dollar, the equivalent of 400 million gold marks. Now, until the Rentenmark was actually issued, the Reichsbank was entitled to continue to discount Treasury bills and print and put into circulation the equivalent amount — which it did to the tune of another 30 trillions.

The authorities, however, realised that if the speculators unleashed an all-out assault on the mark with the paper marks printed between 12th and 15th November there was a danger that any hope of stabilisation would be ruined for good. Therefore, they had recourse to a seemingly paradoxical stratagem. They precipitated the collapse of the mark by raising the rate of the dollar on the Berlin Exchange to 840 milliards on 13th November, to 1,260 on the 14th, to 2,520 on the 15th, and finally to 4·2 billions on 20th November. This was the rate at which the mark was finally stabilised — exactly 1 billion times the rate of the dollar in 1914. One gold mark was now worth 1 billion paper marks, or a "billmark" as it was picturesquely called. This was the rate at which the Rentenmark was fixed in relation to the old money. But the real value of the money in circulation, still 400 million gold marks on 12th November, was reduced by the 15th to only 156 million gold marks; and that was the measure by which the fangs of the speculators, the potential buyers of dollars, were drawn. After that date, with the ban on the discounting of more Treasury bonds, the printing presses of the Reichsbank were condemned to idleness.

Another danger stemmed from the potential further printing of emergency money, which would eventually come out via the Reichsbank in the form of paper money and reinforce the armoury of the speculators. As Schacht himself tells, he made himself very unpopular with the local government bodies and his old friends, the industrialists, who had been resorting to the issue of emergency money in order to finance on a lavish scale their not always very sound investments: it was simply decreed that, with effect from 17th November, the Reichsbank would not accept any more emergency notes and would, on the contrary, insist on selling back those emergency notes still in its coffers. So this was another barrier against the speculators.

These measures took some time to mature, and the mark continued to fall. On 26th November the dollar rate reached 11 billion marks in Cologne and a little less in New York.

But judgement day was coming for the speculators. Indeed, it came on the day they had to settle those debts they had contracted by continuing to buy forward dollars; to be precise, at the end of the month. The dollars had to be paid for with the only legal tender in existence — paper marks. Rentenmarks were not permitted in occupied territory like Cologne, the home of the speculators' orgies, nor abroad.

The speculators were squeezed. They had to sell their dearly-bought dollars to the Reichsbank at the official rate of 4·2 billion marks to the dollar. By the beginning of December this quotation prevailed everywhere, and the Reichsbank had accumulated a sizable hoard of foreign currency (200 million gold marks). This battle in defence of the currency was won; the speculators had burned their fingers. They had lost millions and learned a lesson.

Another battle followed shortly afterwards.

The Rentenmark credit of 1,200 million which the Reich had been granted in November was quickly approaching exhaustion by December. It had been spent on the regular expenses of the administration; the number of unemployed was still very large and involved the paying out of high unemployment benefits. Altogether the Reich seemed to be broke again and approached the Rentenbank for a further credit of 400 million Rentenmarks. The reply was a flat refusal. To comply with the request might have spelled disaster. Moreover, as it turned out, it was not really necessary and standing firm was not just obstinacy, it was fully justified.

It was justified because, in the meantime, the Draconian measures taken to achieve an equilibrium in the Reich's income and expenditure had begun to show results. Tax payments, now in stable money and coming in without undue delay, were gradually increasing. The pruning of the apparatus of the administration, with the consequent reduction in personnel and their salaries, reduced expenses. By the end of the year the budget was not yet balanced, but it was on the way to that goal.

Meanwhile the German economy, and along with it the condition of the people, began to recover from the plight of the Inflation. Prices, which even in real terms had risen in the last phases of the Inflation to great heights, began to come down as a direct consequence of the

availability of stable money: there was no longer any
need to apply the surcharges for the "depreciation risk".
At the same time, wages and salaries improved. The
number of fully unemployed more than halved, dropping
from 1·5 million in January to 700,000 in April;
short-time working ceased almost completely. Buying
food was no longer a problem, as the producers were only
too eager to sell it for the new, good money; people at
long last were able to buy new clothes. The wheels of
industry turned more quickly, trade and production
revived. There was a mood of elation abroad. In the
words of one man, "Now when I see a thousand-mark
note I take my hat off!" For Mrs Barten, who had cried
because she could not afford to have her shoes heeled
and because her husband lacked the price of a tram
ticket, it was indeed a miracle.

> I remember so well the moment when a hundred
> marks were a hundred marks. We had it in a little
> iron box and you cannot imagine what it was like. It
> was like a miracle — that we could actually save and
> put something by. I remember the feeling of having
> just one Rentenmark to spend. I bought a small tin
> breadbin. Just to buy something that had a price tag
> on for *one mark* was so exciting.

In a way, though, the small figures were deceptive and
constituted a dangerous temptation. They concealed the
fact that, in real terms, they were much more precious
than the millions and billions of paper marks. The
money madness that the latter had produced somehow
lingered on and clouded the value judgement of ordinary
people, made them willing to pay substantially high
prices. For instance, W.G. remembers,

213

We bought newspapers freely—why continue in the good new days the old habit of sharing papers with a number of other people — regardless of the fact that the cost was actually very high. Some years later the director of a great publishing house confessed to me that when, after the Inflation, they had to establish the sale price in pfennig, they just "thought of a number" without realising that the price was in fact pretty high, and they made quite disproportionately high profits.

The timing of the appearance of the Rentenmark — in November — actually saved one man from bankruptcy. He had a dress business and, because he could not get the cloth to replace his stock, was on the brink of ruin. But some years earlier he had put money into a seed business on the side. He lived in Tübingen, where this was a local industry. The seeds, of course, were collected in the summer and put into packets. Before they came to be sold in the spring, stabilisation had taken place and customers paid for them in Rentenmarks. It saved him.

A dramatic example of the impact of the new stable currency on the individual was given by Mrs Barten, whose "inflation baby" had to lie in a borrowed cradle.

I wanted so badly to have a second child and my husband said it was impossible as long as the Inflation lasted. How would we feed it? When stabilisation came I said, "Now I can have my second child." We always used to say we ought to have called him Hjalmar after Dr Schacht!

But, as the winter went on, some ominous signs appeared, and a new and final battle for stability loomed on the horizon. The 1,200 million Rentenmarks granted

214

by the Rentenbank had been an absolute necessity for the credit-starved German economy. But gradually the credit policy, perhaps under the influence of the general euphoria which stabilisation had created, became more liberal, too liberal, and by the end of March the total credit had reached 2,000 million and there were signs that some of it was again being used for hoarding foreign currency. Owing to greater consumption and imports of foreign goods, the balance of trade got deeply into the red; domestic prices began to rise; in the foreign exchange markets the value of the German currency deteriorated. The word *Rentenmarkinflation* was bandied about; speculation began to rear its ugly head — the credits that businessmen were able to obtain allowed them to hoard foreign currency instead of selling it to the Reichsbank and thus keeping up the price of the mark.

In April 1924 Dr Schacht, who, as one observer charitably remarks, had been preoccupied with other business, finally devoted his full attention to this unhealthy state of affairs — with a vengeance. On 7th April the blow fell. No such half-measures as raising the bank rate to make credit more expensive. Instead, there was a strict ban on the granting of credit by the Reichsbank (whose President was now Dr Schacht; he had succeeded Dr Havenstein after the latter's timely death on 20th November 1923, the day when the paper mark sank to its lowest on the Berlin Exchange). Dr Schacht wanted to teach the speculators, indeed the whole of big business, not to ask for excessive credits and then speculate with them, at the expense of the common weal and in defiance of the official monetary policy. If they needed money they must liquidate their hoards of goods and, above all, of foreign currency.

The old shibboleth of the Reichsbank under

Havenstein — that it was its sacred duty to provide the economy with all the means of payment — was now finally buried by Havenstein's successor. Now the Reichsbank had won its battle and shown that it was stronger than big business and would henceforward impose its will on it.

It has been estimated that during the Inflation German big business had tucked away abroad the tidy sum of 1,500 million dollars. The hoard, the accumulation of which had drained away so much life blood from the German economy, now came back — or at least part of it did — to support the German currency. This continued to remain stable for many years.

Meanwhile another step was taken to liquidate the legacy of the Inflation and to make good, although on a modest scale, the damage it had inflicted on so many people. The legislation, concerning the "revaluation" of the claims of those who had suffered from the melting away of their capital as a result of the depreciation of the currency, was finalised in July 1925.

The German Supreme Court, on 29th November 1923, had broken with the principle "mark equals mark" simply by deciding that the payment of debts incurred in old marks by corresponding amounts of depreciated paper marks was not a proper discharge. Had this rule been applied uniformly to all paper-mark debts, the ensuing legal free-for-all might well have led to a tremendous upheaval with unforeseeable consequences, possibly doing more harm than good.

The aim of the new legislation was, therefore, to define and limit the rights of creditors in a realistic way. It consisted of two Acts of Parliament of 16th July 1925, one concerning the revaluation of mortgages and similar claims, the other concerning the redemption of Reich, provincial and other public loans. The details of these laws, including the regulations on procedure, are highly complicated, and it took several years and the efforts of entire armies of lawyers to sort them out with, on the whole, equitable results.

The first Act of Parliament fixed the normal rate of revaluation for mortgages and similar rights at 25 per cent of the original gold value, to be repaid not before 1st January 1932 and in the meantime bearing interest rising gradually from 1·2 to 5 per cent. For industrial debentures and similar securities the rate of revaluation was 15 per cent; for certain other claims such as savings bank credits, life insurance claims, and so forth, a pool of the debtors' assets was to be formed for distribution among the creditors.

The other Act of Parliament fixed the normal rate of revaluation for Reich and other securities at 2·5 per cent, establishing a redemption fund for the benefit of such security holders. Holders of securities acquired before 1st July 1920 were entitled to participate in the distribution of the redemption fund by way of a lottery right. This meant that over a period of 30 years lots would be drawn, and the winners would receive 12·5 per cent of the normal value of their securities, plus interest. However, persons with very small incomes would be paid a modest annuity.

There was in both Acts a host of provisions regarding hardship claims, time limits, the treatment of debts already repaid in devalued money, and other qualifications and modifications of the basic rules, quite apart from the regulation for procedure.

In 1927, Herbert Hochfeld, by then a young law graduate serving his apprenticeship in the law courts, was attached to one of the revaluation tribunals. By a curious coincidence, the farmer for whom he had worked early in the Inflation was called before it.

> One of the cases I came across was my old employer, the farmer who had acquired this agricultural empire and who now had to appear before the tribunal to repay some of his mortgages. He had obviously built up his estate by borrowing money from people less intelligent than himself and turning it into real values and then repaying his debts in devalued money. Now according to the revaluation laws he had to pay 25 per cent of the gold-mark value of those old debts. He had already paid off quite a few of them, because he said to the judges at the tribunal, "Gentlemen, it is completely immaterial to me what you consider I should pay. You might make it a million marks, or a 100,000 marks or 10,000 marks. I can't pay anything at all. I just haven't got any money left." In spite of the fact that it had been a huge estate, with rolling-stock and ships and everything, the whole thing had just burst like a soap bubble.

It would go far beyond the scope of this book to illustrate all the details of this legislation. But, on the whole, it was a reasonably fair solution of the problem. Of course, those who had lost heavily in consequence of the Inflation recovered only a fraction of their losses; in the case of the holders of government securities and the like, a very small fraction indeed. But contrasting interests had to be balanced somehow, and circumstances, in any case, made it impossible fully to restore the *status quo* — that is, the situation that had prevailed before the war. For the war and its aftermath had made

Germany a much poorer country, and somebody had to bear the burden.

It has been said with some justification that, had the middle classes not suffered their inflationary losses, they would have had to pay very heavy, perhaps confiscatory, taxes. The Inflation was a form of taxation, and the effect of the new laws was, so to speak, to lighten the tax burden.

Whatever the arguments for or against the fairness of the revaluation, its overriding merit was the contribution it made to the liquidating of the Inflation and the healing of the collective trauma it had caused. To be sure, the old grievances and the material distress were not eliminated, but they were at least alleviated, and a modicum of well-being was restored to those who had suffered so much.

Besides creating capital resources, albeit in a modest way, revaluation was an important element in the revival of confidence: the State, which had been playing havoc with the fortunes of its citizens, had now proved to some degree that it knew its responsibilities toward them and, implicitly, given a promise that such a state of affairs would not be permitted again.

Indeed, confidence had been the essential ingredient of the whole process, ultimately assuring the success of the Rentenmark and the stabilisation of the currency. The elaborate way in which the Rentenmark was created was determined not only by the technicalities of high finance, but also, and mainly, by the psychological factor of gaining the confidence and trust of the public at large in the new currency.

Until then, the mark had been generally mistrusted, and this situation had been responsible for the frantic determination to spend money, to exchange it immediately for *Sachwerte,* and, thus, for the enormous velocity of the circulation. Once confidence was restored, people no longer felt the need to spend, and saving became possible, indeed desirable; the new money was gladly accepted and held until it was really needed for purchases. Thus, even the increased amounts of money brought into circulation did not necessarily constitute a serious danger for the currency.

To sum up, if the issue of Inflation was decided by the struggle between those who were in favour and those against, the latter had come to represent the overwhelming majority. Among them were counted the ordinary people and, as exemplified by Helfferich's initiative, all-important sections of society that had previously stood in the way of stabilisation.

So the struggle for stability was concentrated mainly on the two remaining danger spots: the deficit spending by the Reich and the onslaught of the speculators. The action taken consisted of a denial of excessive credits to the Reich and a limitation of the issue of Rentenmarks, so helping towards the balancing of the budget; and a squeeze against other would-be borrowers, who were thus forced to bring into circulation their own hoards of foreign currencies, so strengthening the mark in the exchange markets.

This struggle was conducted with ruthless determination by the men in charge, conscious that they had the backing of the public and were acting for the common weal. It is not surprising that the restrictive measures taken were not popular in all quarters, and Dr Schacht speaks of the fury he aroused among those who, as he said, "had regarded him as one of themselves". But he remained firm and did not betray his trust.

By a historical coincidence, the stabilisation of the

currency was accompanied by the stabilisation of political life. The incipient Nazi movement, which had fed on the turbulence and misery of economic chaos, seemed to be extinguished forever when, within a few days of the issue of the Rentenmark, Hitler made his abortive bid for power. It was almost as if everything was coming right at once for Germany. W.G. was well placed to savour the moment to the full:

It was a happy coincidence that I was in Munich when the Inflation ended, happy because this fact heightened the sensation of the miraculous and indelibly impressed it on my memory. On 9th November 1923, I had stood in a Munich street watching the Army and police taking up positions against the putschists, and had heard the gunfire that stopped Hitler and his henchmen in their march and signalled the collapse of the putsch. The very real fears of political disaster and direct and personal danger, the doom-laden atmosphere of the preceding days and weeks were dissipated at a stroke. It was as though, in the classical manner, a farce — and the collapse of the putsch had many aspects of a farce — had relieved the tension of the tragedy previously performed.

I felt on top of the world, the miracle had happened, the refrain of an old student song seemed appropriate and had come true: *"hic finis est curarum"* — this is the end of all worries.

The change seemed to call for a celebration. I decided to go to the opera. I put on my 8 million mark dinner-jacket complete with boiled shirt and stiff collar — it was quite ludicrous in the back row of the stalls, and anyhow nobody bothered to dress in

221

those days — but I thought that the occasion called for that gesture.

After the show I went on to one of the more elegant cafés of the town. I only ordered a pot of tea, but I felt good, just like the olden days of solid affluence. My feelings reached their zenith when it came to paying the bill.

I had managed to get hold of a couple of small denomination gold-loan certificates, the stable money that preceded the issue of the Rentenmark; they had been rare and I had hoarded them carefully. Now that the Rentenmark began to flow, there was no longer any reason to preserve them. So I pulled out of my note-case the piece of paper on which was written "One Tenth of a Dollar", or 42 pfennig, paid and departed proudly. The sensation of handling and getting without difficulty value for this money bearing one or two digits was indescribable; it gave a sense of security, prosperity, real happiness. There was, as Hans Fallada put it, "magic in these low figures" — a symbol of the miracle.

The term "miracle of the Rentenmark" is usually dismissed somewhat haughtily by the pundits: there was nothing more to it than sound financial policies. Perhaps this was so, but the confidence underlying all these measures, which would have come to naught if that confidence had, at any moment, given place to panic, was itself really something miraculous.

The public's confidence was created by the conviction that the Rentenmark was backed by land and industrial property, and this, in the public's mind, was accepted as a *Sachwert*, as stable value. There was also the relief that something new had replaced the discredited paper mark and the equally discredited Reichsbank, that the "printing press has stopped".

But the main basis of the confidence was an irrational, almost blind, faith in the new currency. Quite simply, the German people *wanted* to believe in it — and they did.

The backing of the Rentenmark and the Rentenbank, the general charge on industry and agriculture, has been called "fictitious", because it could not be converted into cash or used abroad; indeed, the whole stabilisation was accused of being "a dramatic though legitimate confidence trick, a well-meant bluff". It could perhaps be considered a confidence trick, in the sense that by some clever device confidence was restored. But was it a confidence trick in the sense of a trickster's *abusing* his victims' confidence? Was it a fraud? Or was it a miracle?

In Bernard Shaw's *St Joan,* one of the characters says, "Frauds deceive. An event which creates faith does not deceive: therefore it is not a fraud but a miracle." There could be no better definition of what happened in Germany when the Rentenmark was devised and issued: it was an event that created faith.

Chapter 9

The Road Back

The final seal on the stabilisation of the German currency was set by the Dawes Plan. This consisted of a number of agreements concluded in London on 30th August 1924, between the Allies and Germany, and was concerned with the problems of the payment of reparations and Germany's financial and economic position.

Some outward aspects of the plan were significant. The United States had taken an active interest in this European problem, as is shown by the fact that an American banker, General Charles G. Dawes (later a Vice-President of the U.S.A), gave his name to the plan. The new French Premier, Edouard Herriot, proved to be a man of a much more conciliatory frame of mind than his predecessor, Raymond Poincaré. And in Great Britain Ramsay MacDonald had become Prime Minister. A supporter of international understanding, he was instrumental in overcoming some critical moments in the course of the Dawes Plan Conference in London.

At the suggestion of the President of the United States,

the Reparations Commission, on 30th November 1923, set up two committees of experts. The first, under the chairmanship of Dawes, was to investigate the situation and prospects of Germany's financial and monetary condition; the second, under Mr Reginald McKenna, was to investigate the amount of German assets abroad and the possibility of repatriating them.

When the Dawes Committee, in the course of its labours, visited Berlin in February 1924, it found (in the words of a German commentator, Carl Bergmann) "its task almost accomplished", meaning that stabilisation of the currency and balancing of the budget had proved feasible. Thus it only remained for the committee to give its opinion as to the ability of Germany, on the basis of its financial and economic situation at this point, to discharge its reparations obligations.

The Dawes Committee reported in April 1924 that — to put it succinctly and in very general terms — with a stable currency and a balanced budget, and provided that the economic and financial unity of the Reich, severed by the Ruhr occupation, was restored, the Reich would be able to find the means for paying reparations. But, in view of the preceding ravages of the Inflation, it needed a respite; and consequently, for the first year of the scheme, the sum paid should only be 1,000 million gold marks, of which only 200 million were to be found by Germany, the rest being provided by an international loan. This would also help the stability of the mark. In succeeding years the annual repayments should gradually rise from 1,200 millions to 2,500 millions and then continue on that scale. But a final sum and the duration of the annuities were not stated. The German commitments would be secured by such guarantees as charges on the railways and industry, and controls on revenues from some specific taxes and duties.

A new and very important principle was introduced. Though the committee assumed that Germany, once its freedom of action was restored by economic reunion with the Ruhr, would have the economic strength to find the amounts of reparations payments laid down in the plan, it realised that actually to transfer them, to send the money out of the country, might create great difficulties, even ruin the balance of payments and the currency. This danger was to be averted by an elaborate system, the central point of which was the institution of a reparations agent; payment into the agent's account would in itself be considered the discharge of the Reich's obligations. It was then up to the agent and a special committee to decide to what extent these sums could be converted into foreign moneys without damaging the stability of the German currency.

On the day the Dawes Plan agreements were signed, 30th August 1924, Germany, in deference to the wishes of the Dawes Committee, adopted new monetary laws, which established a new currency, the Reichsmark. This was now the only official currency. It was the final burial of the old paper mark, and the Rentenmark too was to be liquidated: they were both to disappear completely from circulation and make room for the new Reichsmark.

The acceptance of the Dawes Plan — although it was controversial inside Germany and sharply attacked again by right-wing circles — had cleared the air and created a new and hopeful atmosphere. It had largely taken the reparations problem out of politics. It had led to the restoration of the Ruhr to the German economy. It had drawn the Americans back into Europe, and they showed a confidence in the economic future of Europe, and Germany in particular, much needed to raise the low spirits on this side of the Atlantic. At that time Germany could do with an injection of confidence.

It is necessary here briefly to return to the events of 7th April 1924, when Dr Schacht ruthlessly crushed the danger of a new inflation by applying Draconian credit restrictions. It was a deflationary policy of the classic kind: he had to sacrifice the booming of the economy for the sake of the stability of the currency.

As credit became scarce interest rates climbed, the prices of stocks and shares dropped and so did commercial prices. Unemployment again rose, short-time working spread. There were insolvencies and bankruptcies on a disquieting scale. But the trade balance improved and even went for a time into the black. Foreign currency, at the official rate, became freely available.

Yet it can safely be said that, with the memories of the dark days of the Inflation still fresh in the public mind, this situation, however much hardship it brought to many individuals, was accepted by the community at large as a lesser evil.

Their unbroken confidence was re-echoed abroad, and this was translated into a generous flow of foreign loans into Germany, for both private business and public bodies such as municipalities, the provinces, and the Reich itself. Some of these credits were short-term; some were not used to the best advantage.

It was estimated that between 1924 and 1930 more than 20,000 million gold marks in foreign loans poured into Germany. This gigantic amount of debts, whilst being only a temporary relief, was a constant danger, and when the world crisis of the thirties led to withdrawal of these credits it was an essential contributory factor to the economic disasters that then befell Germany. But that is another story.

For the time being, however, the credits helped to revive the German economy and until June 1925 brought a period of growing prosperity. Unemployment fell, production rose, interest rates dropped, as did the number of bankruptcies.

But in June 1925 this boom again came to an end. It was not a currency crisis but a genuine economic recession, which lasted far into the year 1926, driving up the unemployment figure to a maximum of about 3 million in mid-1926; once again there was a spate of collapses of many business enterprises. But it was — to use the word of the moment — an "epuration" crisis: the liquidation, postponed for a short period in the preceding months, of the legacy of the Inflation.

It is characteristic that the lion's share of the businesses that fell victim to that crisis were the overblown and inefficient conglomerations that the Inflation tycoons had built up, hastily, improvidently and without regard for the general health of the economy. Foremost among them, the Stinnes empire collapsed, and many others of that type more or less shared its fate, while the old-established enterprises survived. This "purge" was in itself a natural and healthy development, and it was perhaps due to the realisation of this fact that the main sufferers — the working classes — bore it with fortitude.

Indeed, during the year 1926 their patience began to be rewarded. Various factors contributed to the return of better conditions. As the old, inflation-bred organisation of industry disappeared, the capital provided by foreign loans, or a good deal of it, was more wisely used by the industrial enterprises — not just to enlarge their plants, but also to rationalise the productive process and make it more efficient; for with American money, American know-how also was imported.

Another factor worth mentioning is the British coal strike of 1926, which gave the German coal industry, and subsequently also the iron and steel industry, an enormous boost, enabling them to penetrate markets that until then had been the preserve of their British competitors.

Another phenomenon of the post-Inflation period, and one that caused the authorities to intervene by raising the fee for a passport to 500 gold marks, was what Bresciani-Turroni rather unkindly calls "the craze for foreign travel which suddenly possessed certain classes of the German people". It was not just a craze, as W.G., who experienced it, testifies:

> It was the return to the old era of prosperity and stability when the "Italian Journey" was the pride and birthright of the educated middle class, a symbol of their position in civilised society. I went off for a whirlwind tour of North Italy with a few friends of my own age. Appropriately we started the journey in a fourth-class compartment to the frontier; changed there to first class; spent a couple of days in the dreamed-of Italian sunshine of Lake Garda; stopped at Milan in the Hotel Continentale, and finished with two days at the Danieli in Venice. And then home again.
>
> It was arrogance, vanity, snobbishness, but it was above all the symbol that the Inflation was over, that the nightmare was over, the portent of better days to come. It was, of course, an illusion.

A sad little note from Mrs Barten echoes this thought:

"Only by 1928 were we recovered enough to start going on holidays again — and that was only for four years, because the Nazis began in East Prussia in 1932."

The whirlwind had blown itself out. In the ravaged landscape of the national life over which the storm had passed, people had begun to put their lives together again. But, for unthinking youth, the upside-down world of the Inflation had been a time of excitement, of the breakdown of order, of the erosion of parental discipline. For many young people the end of the Inflation was not a positive return to normality but a negative return to dull routine. It was a dangerous portent for the future of Germany. Young Lisa Frank, settling down on her stool to the now humdrum work of a clerk at the Reichsbank, speaks for her generation:

> The old marks were burnt in the courtyard of the bank. The books were changed — it was all very easy. But I found it afterwards very boring. When it was normal I didn't like it. I just didn't like it. I was young then — 22 years old. The work was boring, everything was boring. It had been so exciting — just to throw the money away on things. One can learn that money really just isn't anything.

Chapter 10

Hitler in the Wings

Under the influence of the Inflation the physical and intellectual conditions of the German people had deteriorated; moral standards had been debased; the old virtues of thrift, of hard and constructive work had given way to a spirit of rapacity and greed and a fever of speculation. It was only natural that, with so many spheres of social life changing to the point of revolution, politics could not remain unaffected.

An economic and social phenomenon of the scale of the Inflation was bound to affect German politics in a multitude of ways. It led to changes of government, influenced elections, caused strikes often heavily coloured by political aims, largely determined fiscal and financial policies and played an important part in shaping German foreign policy.

In fact, to give a complete analysis of the political effects of the Inflation would amount to writing the political history of Germany during the period, which is not within the scope of this book.

What is relevant is to consider whether and to what

extent the great German Inflation was responsible for the destruction of the ideals of freedom and democracy embodied in the Weimar Republic, and to assess the claim, which many people make, that Hitler was the foster child of the Inflation.

This claim is often flatly denied on the plausible grounds that Hitler did not come to power until more than nine years after the end of the Inflation, and that, consequently, the Nazi ascent to the status and power of a mass movement must be ascribed to the great depression of the years 1929–33, with the ensuing wave of unemployment and distress. In the absence of the depression, it is contended, German society would have been able to recuperate from both the material and the psychological ravages of the Inflation. If there is any link between the Inflation and Nazism, it is that the very fear of renewed inflation led the German governments before Hitler to adopt those deflationary policies which, if they did not actually produce the desperate state of the economy, failed to remedy it.

The argument is valid as far as it goes. It is of course true that only in the wake of the great depression, after the general election of September 1930, did the Nazis enter the political arena of the German Parliament as a large party, in fact the second largest in the House, and then continued their triumphal advance.

It is also true that the years of comparative prosperity that followed the end of the Inflation coincided with a cooling-down of political passions.

But this leaves out of account the fact that the Inflation and the conditions it created provided the soil and climate in which the seed of Hitlerism was nurtured, preserved and enabled to grow when the favourable circumstances of the depression supervened.

234

Whether the grievances, the envy and the wounded vanity of the classes hardest hit by the Inflation were entirely justified, and whether their shift to the extreme Right was but a perversion of nationalism, which had been the traditional creed of at least some sectors of these classes, are moot points. Though impoverished they remained essentially bourgeois, hated being proletarians in the economic sense and disdained socialism. But their tolerance, human compassion and respect for the individual withered, together with their former feeling of security, under the impact of their seemingly undeserved distress. They came to hate the new democratic State, which was grey and colourless and deprived them even of the outward trappings of their prestige and standing in society. The upsurge of nationalism offered them new symbols, and enabled them to preserve their white-collar mentality while expressing hostility towards the ugly face of capitalism, especially when propaganda vested it with a Jewish mask.

Thus the Nazi party was to become a magnet for them, however slow the process of attraction.

Hitler realised early that their misery was his best recruiting officer. In a speech he made during the Inflation (quoted by Konrad Heiden) he said,

And what if even greater misery descended on us? Let us have misery! . . . the greatest misfortune would be so-called prosperity . . . If the horrified people notice that they can starve on billions, they must arrive at the conclusion, "We will no longer submit to a state which is built on the swindling idea of the majority; we want dictatorship."

235

The Great Inflation

Misery engendered by inflation was obviously the revolutionary situation Hitler needed for his aims. Indeed, his first attempt at gaining power, the Munich Putsch of 9th November 1923, came to naught partly because one of the potential confederates, the industrialist Friedrich Minoux, considered that there was not yet enough misery and distress about to guarantee the success of a rising.

Significantly, the failure of the Putsch coincided with the stabilisation of the German currency, which brought to an end that particular source of misery. But the seed had been sown. Hitler just had to wait for new misery, resentment and insecurity, and a readiness on the part of the people to embrace new ideologies, before it could come to fruition.

The Inflation also provided, in a positive way, ammunition for the onslaught on the Republic. As has already been discussed, the men who had accumulated huge fortunes during the Inflation devoted large amounts of money to propaganda against the régime, fostering a nationalism which, though it did not yet fully identify itself with Nazism, was its best ally and pacemaker.

At the same time, the fighting funds of the workers' organisations that might have financed counter-propaganda had been depleted by the collapse of the currency. The expropriated middle classes became a receptive target for nationalist propaganda.

It is difficult to show by mere figures that the Inflation rendered the German people more susceptible to the blandishments of nationalist and National-Socialist ideologies. One pointer, however, is provided by the fluctuations of the vote in German general elections during the relevant years, although, naturally, the Inflation was only one element of many that motivated the electorate.

In the elections for the National Assembly in January 1919, the three parties unreservedly supporting the democratic system and the Republic — the Social Democratic, Democratic and Centre parties — had obtained an absolute majority in the Assembly. The value of the mark was at that time still about one half of its pre-war value. The next elections, for the new Reichstag, took place in June 1920, when the mark was worth only about one tenth of its value before the war. In this election the republican-democratic coalition lost its majority, *never to regain it*.

The subsequent elections in May 1924 took place, it is true, after the stabilisation of the currency, but with the effects of the Inflation still a dominating factor in the minds of the electorate. For the first time, members of the Nazi Party were elected to the Reichstag — 32 of them. The Nationalist Party, with 106 members, became the strongest party in the House. Its success was characteristically due to its demagogic propaganda, which promised the victims of the Inflation 100 per cent compensation.

At the same time, the Democratic Party, standing for the ideas and ideals of the solid, liberal and progressive middle class, was reduced to 28 seats and was indeed on the way to gradual effacement.

In the 1928 elections, after some years of relative stability and prosperity, there was, it is true, a swing back from the extreme Right to the Left, but one fact seems to be significant: there was no massive revival of support for the Democratic Party (who obtained only 25 seats). There was also an upsurge of splinter parties, designed to accommodate the disgruntled middle class. These parties were by no means wholeheartedly democratic and were easy prey for the Nazis in the future.

It is perhaps fair to deduce from these facts alone that the decomposition of the middle class and its alienation from liberal ideas — both products of the Inflation — had come to stay, with all that this augured for the future. But even if this reasoning may seem too speculative, anyone who lived through that period of German history knows that its conclusions are no mere fantasies. As Stefan Zweig wrote, "Nothing made the German people so embittered, so raging with hatred, so ripe for Hitler, as the Inflation." Many minds were moulded by the experience of the Inflation into a Nazi mentality, and though this remained latent in many, it only needed the trauma of the great depression to set these forces loose.

One remembers fellow students, the resentful sons and daughters of impoverished victims of the Inflation, who saw themselves deprived of their birthright to a good life, poor, facing a drab existence and an uncertain future. It was difficult for anybody not to be attracted by the new ideologies, while the comradeship of the Nazi troops, the uniforms, the flags and the marching were an all-too-alluring substitute for the things they and their parents had lost during the Inflation.

They withdrew from their old friends more and more into the Nazi orbit, a bit shamefacedly at first perhaps, not showing their swastikas and uniforms and behaving correctly when, as was inevitable, they came into contact with others. But they were true pillars of the movement, coming into the open as Hitler's fortunes prospered, and often emerging as the rabid and uncompromising cadres so characteristic of the Nazis once they had actually achieved power.

The parents, the older generation, followed suit, if less

exuberantly. For a long time they continued to read the liberal press, but ceased to accept its progressive views. They replaced the flag of the Republic, not immediately with the swastika, but for an intermediate period with the flag of the Kaiser's Germany. They did not burn their books by Jewish authors immediately, but pushed them to the back of the shelves. "How was it possible", asks Arnold Brecht in his memoirs, "to convince a nation of the values of democracy in the face of such a witches' Sabbath?"

The traumatic experience of the Inflation, the impoverishment, the proletarianisation, the loss of status and influence, all had a lasting effect on the middle classes and especially on their sons and daughters. Their material, political and spiritual values were destroyed; the quality of life was changed.

The Nazi party was waiting for them, offering a safe haven, a promise of stability.

It was a longing for security, the legacy of the catastrophic experience of the Inflation, that determined the attitude of many Germans when the world depression and the economic crisis in Germany confronted them with new problems and choices.

They chose Hitler.

List of Sources

ANGELL, J. W., *The Recovery of Germany*, 1929.

BERGMANN, C., *Der Weg der Reparation*, 1926.

BONN, M. J., *Wandering Scholar*, 1949.

BRACHER, K. D., *Die Auflösung der Weimarer Republik*, 1957.

BRECHT, A., *Aus nächster Nähe*, 1966.

BRESCIANI-TURRONI, C., *The Economics of Inflation*, 1953.

BUCK, P. S., *How it Happens: Talk about the German People, 1914–1933, with Erna von Pustau*, 1947.

CASTELLAN, G., *L'Allemagne de Weimar, 1918–1933*, 1969.

CLARKE, S. V. O., "The Reconstruction of the International Monetary System. The Attempts of 1922 and 1933" in *Princeton Studies in International Finance* no. 31.

VISCOUNT D'ABERNON, *German Currency, its Collapse and Recovery*, 1926.

VISCOUNT D'ABERNON, *Portraits and Appreciations*, 1931.

The Great Inflation

VISCOUNT D'ABERNON, *An Ambassador of Peace*, 1929.

DEUERLEIN, E. (ed.), *Der Hitler-Putsch*, 1962.

Die Deutsche Mark von 1914–1924. Von 1 Mark bis 100 Billionen (no date).

ELSTER, K., *Von der Mark zur Reichsmark*, 1928.

EULENBURG, F., "Die Sozialen Wirkungen der Währungsverhältnisse" in *Jahrbücher für Nationalökonomie und Statistik*, 1924.

EYCK, E., *Geschichte der Weimarer Republik*, 1954.

FALLADA, H., *Wolf unter Wölfen*, 1937.

FISCHER, W., *Die Wirtschaftspolitik Deutschlands 1918–1945*, 1961.

FLENLEY, R., *Modern German History*, 1964.

FRIEDENSBURG, F., *Die Weimarer Republik*, 1957.

FRIEDMAN, I. S., *Inflation, a World-wide Disaster*, 1973.

FÜRSTENBERG, H., *Erinnerungen*, 1965.

GAETTENS, R., *Inflationen*, 1955.

GAY, P., *Weimar Culture*, 1969.

GEYER, C., *Die Verderber Deutschlands*, 1924.

GRUNBERGER, R., *A Social History of the Third Reich*, 1974.

HAHN, A. L., *Fünfzig Jahre zwischen Inflation und Deflation*, 1963.

HALPERIN, S. W., *Germany Tried Democracy*, 1946.

HARMSSEN, G. W. (ed.), *Reparationen Sozialprodukt Lebensstandard*, 1947.

HEIDEN, K., *Der Führer*, 1944.

HEUSS, Th., *Erinnerungen*, 1963.

JOHNSON, H. G., "Inflation and World Trade: a 'Monetarist' View" in *Journal of World Trade Law* vol. 6, no. 1.

KEYNES, J. M., *The Economic Consequences of the Peace*, 1920.

VON KLASS, G., *Hugo Stinnes*, 1958.

LASSWELL, H. L., *The Analysis of Political Behaviour*, 1949.

LAURSEN, K. and PEDERSEN, J., *The German Inflation 1918–1923*, 1964.

LEWINSOHN, R., *Histoire de l'Inflation*, 1926.

LUTHER, H., *Politiker ohne Partei*, 1960.

MICHAELIS, H., SCHRAEPLER, E., SCHEEL, G. (ed.), *Ursachen und Folgen. Eine Urkunden- und Dokumentensammlung zur Zeitgeschichte*, 1960.

NAPHTALI, F., *Im Zeichen des Währungselends*, 1923.

OSTWALD, H., *Sittengeschichte der Inflation*, 1931.

PINNER, F., *Deutsche Wirtschaftsführer*, 1924.

Verwaltungsbericht der Reichsbank 1922, 1923.

RINGER, F. K. (ed.), *The German Inflation of 1923*, 1969.

ROSENBERG, A., *Geschichte der Deutschen Republik*, 1935.

SCHACHT, H., *Die Stabilisierung der Mark*, 1927.

SCHACHT, H., *My First Seventy-six Years*, 1953.

SCHEELE, G., *The Weimar Republic*, 1946.

SCHOENBERNER, F., *Bekenntnisse eines europäischen Intellektuellen*, 1964.

SCHREIBER, G., *Die Not der deutschen Wissenschaft und der geistigen Arbeiter*, 1923.

SPEER, A., *Die Inflationszeit*, 1933.

STAMPFER, F., *Die vierzehn Jahre der Ersten Deutschen Republik*, 1936.

Statistisches Jahrbuch für das Deutsche Reich, 1921–1924.

STATISTISCHES REICHSAMT, *Zahlen zur Geldentwertung in Deutschland 1914–1923*, 1925.

STOLPER, G., HÄUSER, K., BORCHART, K., *The German Economy, 1870 to the Present*, 1967.

STUCKEN, R., *Deutsche Geld- und Kreditpolitik 1914–1953*, 1953.

UFERMANN, P., *Könige der Inflation*, 1924.

VOCKE, W., *Memoiren*, 1973.

WOOLLCOTT, A., *While Rome Burns*, 1945.

ZUCKMAYER, C., *Als wär's ein Stück von mir*, 1967.

ZWEIG, S., *Die Welt von Gestern*, 1941.

ZWEIG, S., *Die unsichtbare Sammlung*, 1972.

Index

Index